Front cover: A watercolour painting from the fields of Witherhill Farm looking north to Exmoor.

(Thought to be by a friend of Mrs Molly Hare of Ward's Cottage, probably in the 1960s)

'So life was never better than

In nineteen sixty-three

(Though just too late for me) -

Between the end of the Chatterley ban

And the Beatles' first LP'.

An extract from the poem 'Annus Mirabilis' by Philip Larkin

1963

Diary of a Farmer's Son

by Philip George Keen

Samuel George Keen (1922 - 1991)
& Hazel Jane Keen (1921 - 2008)

For Olivia, Josephine and Fraser.

1963
Diary of a Farmer's Son.

Perhaps as a Christmas gift, or as a present for my 13th birthday in December 1962, I was given a 'Letts School-Boys Diary', and during the year of 1963 I managed to keep a record of life at my school and growing up on a family farm in rural North Devon.

My parents, along with my brother Roger and me, moved to Witherhill Farm, High Bickington in early 1956 from Bow, near Crediton in Devon. My other brother Edward was born later, in 1961. Witherhill was a farm of about 70 acres just outside the village of High Bickington. It was a small mixed farm, typical of its time, with poultry, sheep, pigs, cows, and some beef cattle, along with corn and various arable crops.

I first attended the local primary school and later Chulmleigh Secondary School. This involved a bus trip of nearly 10 miles to and from school every day. Apart from everyday events, my diary for 1963 reflects a year of huge social change, from one of the coldest winters in British history through the emergence of popular music and youth culture to the Profumo scandal and the assassination of President Kennedy in the USA. It also records what it was like growing up in rural North Devon as a schoolboy and a new teenager in a fast-changing world.

The following pages show scanned copies of the original pages with a transcription of the entries and extra notes where space allows. Interspersed with them are some short stories and memories of the time, inspired and encouraged by my time with the Shobrooke and Stockleigh Pomeroy Writing Group.

There are also plenty of football results, health updates and weather reports!

Witherhill Farm, High Bickington, Devon.

About a mile from the village of High Bickington, Witherhill Farm is a Grade II listed farmhouse overlooking the Taw valley. In the listing it is described as a "notably comple example of a medieval Devon farmhouse and has been little altered since the 19th century". The earliest parts were said to date from the late 15th or early 16th centuries It was purchased at auction from the Pyncombe Estate in the 1920s by George Pidler and later worked by his son William.

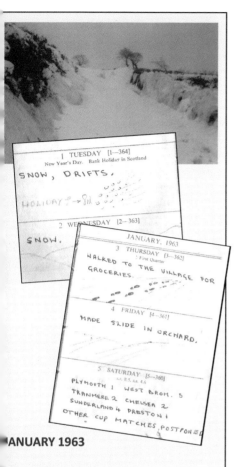

ANUARY 1963

TUESDAY: SNOW, DRIFTS.

WEDNESDAY: SNOW.

THURSDAY: WALKED TO THE VILLAGE OR GROCERIES.

FRIDAY: MADE SLIDE IN ORCHARD.

SATURDAY:

LYMOUTH 1 WEST BROM 5

RANMERE 2 CHELSEA 2

UNDERLAND 4 PRESTON 1

THER CUP MATCHES POSTPONED

The snow came to us late on Boxing Day in 1962: paper-chains still hung on the wall and newly-opened Christmas presents lay under the tree. It came on a bitter east wind, whistling down from the Exmoor hills and against the old farmhouse door. I watched a thin arrow of snow squeeze through a gap in the wood panels of the back door and form on the wall inside. We did not know it then, but we were about to endure the hardest winter in over two hundred years, and the coldest January ever recorded in Britain.

The snow falling on the fields outside would still be there eight weeks later. The rivers, and the sea around the coast, would freeze over. Villages and towns would be cut off for weeks, with severe shortages of food, especially milk and vegetables. Farm animals and wildlife would suffer huge losses. It was thought that half of Britain's birds perished in the bitter cold.

The poet Ted Hughes visited Devon at that time to check on the house in North Tawton that he had lived in with his wife, the writer and poet Sylvia Plath, and their two children. It features in his poem *Robbing Myself.*

"I came over the snow – the packed snow
The ice-glaze hardened and polished,
Slithering the A30, two hundred miles,
The road unnatural and familiar,
A road back into myself"

He describes locking up the sad and silent house and gathering a bag of stored apples and potatoes to take back to London and to Sylvia, unaware she was only weeks away from suicide.

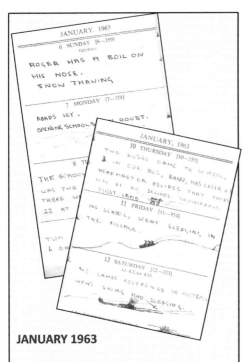

JANUARY 1963

6 SUNDAY: SNOW THAWING.

7 MONDAY: ROADS ICY. OPENING SCHOOLS IN DOUBT.

8 TUESDAY: SCHOOL OPENED, OURS WAS THE ONLY BUS THAT WENT. THERE WERE 5 IN THE BUS, AND 22 AT SCHOOL.

9 WEDNESDAY: TWO BUSES GOT TO SCHOOL, 6 ON OUR BUS, 36 IN SCHOOL.

10 THURSDAY: TWO BUSES CAME TO SCHOOL, 3 IN OUR BUS, BARRY, MRS GREEN AND I. HEADMASTER DECIDES THAT THERE WILL BE NO SCHOOL TOMORROW. FIRST LAMB.

11 FRIDAY: NO SCHOOL, WENT SLEDGING IN THE VILLAGE.

12 SATURDAY: 42 GAMES POSTPONED IN FOOTBALL. WENT SKI-ING AND SLEDGING.

As 1963 began the snow had been falling for a week. It lay in drifts on the frozen hard ground. By then we had to take a sledge and walk to the village shop to load it with groceries, and the heavy grey sky above us seemed close enough to touch as we crunched through the white crust of snow that came up to our knees. The world around was hushed and silent, as if smothered in blankets of white. We thought there would be no chance of the bus getting to school the following week.

On January 8th, however, our intrepid driver, relishing a challenge, pipe fixed in mouth, managed to wrestle our small bus over miles of country roads covered in ice and up to the school gate, only to find it was the only one to get there. The next day two buses got through but still only thirty-six pupils managed to get to school. The following day the timetable was abandoned and it was announced school would be closed. Before going home we sat around the heaters drinking the best hot chocolate I had ever tasted. Back at home our first lamb was born warm and wet into the freezing world.

We children spent the weekend sledging and creating runs in the deep snow. Someone in the village lent us a pair of skis. We seemed not to mind the cold then: fingers numb from holding snowball would be revived in bowls of warm water.

A second lamb came bravely into the world. It was not a good time for them: many were lost that year and sheep, especially on the moors, were buried in deep drifts. Our sheep came down from the fields on their own accord to seek shelter in the orchard nearer the house.

Snow on the fields of Witherhill in 1963.

JANUARY 1963

13 SUNDAY: SNOW STILL ABOUT.

14 MONDAY: SECOND LAMB. PLYMOUTH SIGN P. MCPARLAND.

15 TUESDAY: DAD'S BIRTHDAY. HE WENT TO BARNSTAPLE.

16 WEDNESDAY: MISSED THE BUS. SUNNY. BORROWED HOPKIN'S SLEDGE. BURNLEY BEAT SPURS 3-0! THIRD ROUND CUP.

17 THURSDAY: VERY WINDY AND COLD. 50 IN SCHOOL.

18 FRIDAY: IN SCHOOL WE SAW A FILM. ONLY 3 ON OUR BUS.

19 SATURDAY: SNOW. FELL OFF SLEDGE AT SNAPE HILL.

They must have sensed the bad weather that was to come. It also meant it was easier for us to look after them.

Often in the middle of the night we'd help a ewe struggling to give birth, my father finally pulling the lamb out, yellow and shining with the afterbirth, onto the frozen snow. Weak lambs would be brought inside to lie on old newspapers by the Rayburn and, hopefully, to recover. As the winter wore on foxes became bolder, driven by hunger. We would paint tar on the hedges, and hang oil lamps to deter them, but in the dark night the torchlight would often catch the reflection of a shining pair of eyes. It was said that on Dartmoor starving foxes were hunting in packs, killing weakened sheep.

The water supply for the house was freezing up, so my father set up the old pump in the kitchen that was used before the mains water was connected. There was supposed to be an ancient well under the kitchen floor, and with a few pumps on the handle, clear cold water came gurgling up from the deep, dark earth below.

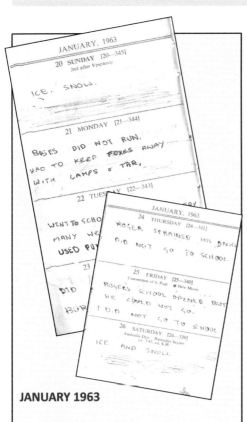

JANUARY 1963

20 SUNDAY: ICE. SNOW.

21 MONDAY: BUSES DID NOT RUN. HAD TO KEEP FOXES AWAY WITH LAMPS AND TAR.

22 TUESDAY: WENT TO SCHOOL, COLD, NOT VERY MANY WENT. USED PUMP FOR WATER.

23 WEDNESDAY: DID NOT GO TO SCHOOL. BURNLEY (0)1 LIVERPOOL(1)1 4ᵗʰ ROUND F.A. CUP.

24 THURSDAY: ROGER SPRAINED HIS ANKLE. DID NOT GO TO SCHOOL.

25 FRIDAY: ROGER'S SCHOOL OPENED BUT HE DID NOT GO. I DID NOT GO TO SCHOOL.

26 SATURDAY: ICE AND SNOW.

NOTES FOR JANUARY 1963:

Football results were mainly of the Devon club Exeter City and Plymouth Argyle and the team started to follow after watching the 1962 Cup Final, Burnley.

3ʳᵈ The shop we walked to was in North Road, High Bickington.

10ᵗʰ The school bus was from Chantry Garage in Atherington. The bus driver was George Trigger. Mrs Green was a school secretary, and Barry was Barry Tapscott.

14ᵗʰ Peter McParland was an international footballer. He played 34 times for Northern Ireland.

15ᵗʰ My father would have been 42 years old on this day.

16ᵗʰ Mr and Mrs Hopkins lived at Nethergrove Farm just up the road.

19ᵗʰ Snape Hill originally belonged to Snape Farm, then farmed by Mr Taverner. It is a steep field, sloping into the road.

22ⁿᵈ There was originally a pump in the kitchen, with a granite trough which was put outside the front door when mains water was connected. A new bathroom was put in upstairs by dividing the end bedroom and creating a window in the wall. The toilet was outside before that.

24ᵗʰ My brother sprained an ankle when his sledge went crashing through the orchard hedge and landed in the road.

28ᵗʰ My nearest grammar school would have been in Barnstaple.

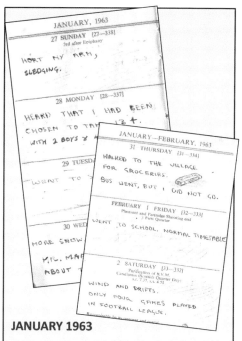

On Friday 1st February, the school was open with a normal timetable, but on the Monday it began to snow heavily again and we were all sent home. By Wednesday the heaviest snows of the winter began to fall with drifts of over 15 feet high, and roads completely vanished from sight. It was, however, a last gasp. Some days later on the 8th the big thaw began, creating the extra hazard of flooding. That weekend on the Sunday I walked across the fields following fox tracks on the snowline that still remained, and into the woods where lumps of snow slumped off low branches and on to the slippery wet earth below. The world seemed to be waking up and shaking off its cold slumber.

That evening, in a house on a London street, still deep in dark despair, the poet Sylvia Plath put out milk and a plate of bread for her two small children, sealed their bedroom door tightly to protect them, and turned on the gas.

Over the next 2 days the weather warmed, snow around the farm dropped off trees and rooftops and the white carpet moved away. It melted quickly across the ground, revealing shining red-brown earth and stones, emerging snowdrops and daffodils, and the bright new, sparkling green grass.

The light was back.

JANUARY 1963

27 SUNDAY: HURT MY ARM, SLEDGING.

28 MONDAY: HEARD THAT I HAD BEEN CHOSEN TO TAKE 13+ WITH 2 BOYS AND 4 GIRLS.

29 TUESDAY: WENT TO SCHOOL.

30 WEDNESDAY: MORE SNOW, BUS DID NOT GO. MR MARSH RANG UP ABOUT THE 13+.

31 THURSDAY: WALKED TO THE VILLAGE FOR GROCERIES. BUS WENT, BUT I DID NOT GO.

FEBRUARY 1963

1 FRIDAY: WENT TO SCHOOL, NORMAL TIMETABLE.

2 SATURDAY: WIND AND DRIFTS. ONLY FOUR GAMES PLAYED IN FOOTBALL LEAGUE.

FEBRUARY 1963

3 SUNDAY: MORE SNOW.

4 MONDAY: WENT TO SCHOOL. BEGAN TO SNOW HARD, SO WE HAD DINNER AND WENT HOME. SO DID ROGER. SLIPPERY.

5 TUESDAY: DID NOT GO TO SCHOOL, SNOW, RAIN AND VERY COLD.

6 WEDNESDAY: DEEP SNOW, BLIZZARDS, DRIFTS, UNBELIEVABLE. ROADS BAD, NO SCHOOL.

7 THURSDAY: FOWL HOUSE FLOODED. MADE SLEDGE TRACK IN SNOW. WENT TO TAYLOR'S LANE, SNOW VERY DEEP.

8 FRIDAY: THAW BEGINS, FLOODS, RAIN. QUEEN TOURS NEW ZEALAND.

9 SATURDAY: SNOW ALMOST GONE. BUT NOT MANY F.A. GAMES PLAYED.
LEICESTER 2 ARSENAL 0
PLYMOUTH 4 MIDDLESBOROUGH 5

FEBRUARY 1963

10 SUNDAY: SNOW AGAIN. WENT FOR A WALK.

11 MONDAY: MANCHESTER UNITED SIGN PAT CRERAND.

12 TUESDAY: WE HAD OUR HAIR CUT. GOT TRANSISTER.

13 WEDNESDAY: THAW.

14 THURSDAY: HAD ANTI-SMOKING LEAFLETS.

15 FRIDAY: SENT AWAY FOR RECORD AND PHOTOS.

16 SATURDAY: MR TAVERNER CAME TO SEE US.

reenleas, Bow, near Crediton, home of my unt Mary and my grandparents. Now emolished, it was formerly known as 'St Martins', and was located opposite Bow ation. The station master who lived there at e time was a Mr Hanton and his family.

grandfather James Pickard at 'Greenleas' ing February 1963.

FEBRUARY 1963

17 SUNDAY: WENT TO GREENLEAS. NEW PULLOVER.

18 MONDAY: LOT OF LAMBS. DROPPED HORACE OUT OF BOWL BUT HE WAS ALRIGHT.

19 TUESDAY: AUNT MARY CAME DOWN BY TRAIN.

20 WEDNESDAY: THRESHING. HAD A BLACK LAMB.

21 THURSDAY: SENT AWAY FOR A COMPETITION. ENGLAND HAVE LOST TEST MATCHES.

22 FRIDAY: CROSS COUNTRY, VERY TOUGH, 30th OUT OF 60. BARRY 2nd. WATCHED FILM AFTER IT.

23 SATURDAY: RECORD CAME. FOOTBALL: H.B. WON, PLYMOUTH LOST. LOT OF LAMBS, WE INJECTED THEM. HELPED WITH STRAW. MARY WENT HOME.

FEBRUARY 1963

24 SUNDAY: PLAYED A BIT OF FOOTBALL. COLD AND CLOUDY.

25 MONDAY: HALF TERM HOLIDAY.

26 TUESDAY: WENT TO SCHOOL. NO PANCAKES.

27 WEDNESDAY: WATCHED P.E. FILM. PLAYED FOOTBALL, HALF-PERIOD.

28 THURSDAY: HOLIDAY. WENT TO INTER-PARTY AT THE CHAPEL. BARRY CAME DOWN.

MARCH 1963

1 FRIDAY: SAW FILM IN SCHOOL (GOOD). RODE BIKE.

2 SATURDAY: FOUND FILM BOX. H.B. WIN 6-5. BURNLEY LOSE, LEICESTER WIN, EXETER WIN, SPURS WIN, PLYMOUTH WIN, SWINDON WIN, TORQUAY DRAW, CHELSEA LOSE. FOX KILLED A LAMB.

NOTES FOR FEBRUARY 1963:

7th Taylor's Lane is a lane running south of the farm from White Bridge on the B3127 to Snape Lane, just above Deep Lane. Much of it was a Green Lane.

8th The Queen and the Duke of Edinburgh visited New Zealand during February.

11th Pat Crerand was a Scottish international footballer signed by Manchester United from Celtic.

16th Mr Taverner lived at Snape Farm.

18th Horace was a pet goldfish won at Barnstaple Fair, and lived to a good age.

Favourite films I saw during the year:
101 DALMATIONS (Walt Disney cartoon),
JULIUS CAESAR (starring Marlon Brando),
IN SEARCH OF THE CASTAWAYS (starring Hayle
Mills and Maurice Chevalier).

Some records I bought during the year: 'GLAD
ALL OVER' The Dave Clark Five, 'TWIST AND
SHOUT' The Beatles, 'SHE LOVES YOU' The
Beatles, 'YOU'LL NEVER WALK ALONE' Gerry
and the Pacemakers, 'BAD TO ME' The Beatle.

Bill Pidler on horseback, in the yard at Witherhill Farm, probably in the 1940s.

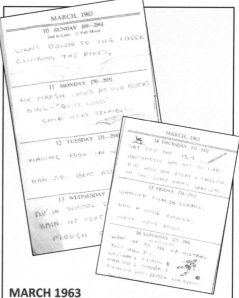

MARCH 1963

3 SUNDAY: 3 LAMBS, 2 DEAD. BROKE
FOOTBALL. DAD CAUGHT A BUZZARD
AND A HARE.

4 MONDAY: EDWARD HAS A COLD. SNOW
STILL ABOUT ON DARTMOOR.

5 TUESDAY: MARY CAME DOWN.

6 WEDNESDAY: PLAY BARNSTAPLE
(AWAY), LEFT HALF. JUNIORS 2-1 WIN
(UNBEATEN) SENIORS 0-4 LOSE.

7 THURSDAY: WENT TO SCHOOL.
WATCHED T.V.

8 FRIDAY: HAD NEW SHOES.

9 SATURDAY: PLAYED FOR H.B. MINORS AT
FREMINGTON - LOSE 4-1. MARY GOES
HOME. FOX HUNTING.
BURNLEY DRAW. MAN. UTD. LOSE.

MARCH 1963

10 SUNDAY: WENT DOWN TO THE COVER
CLIMBING THE DYKES.

11 MONDAY: MR MARSH LOOKS AT OUR
BOOKS, MINE- "QUITE GOOD", SOME
WERE TERRIBLE.

12 TUESDAY: MAKING BOX IN
WOODWORK.
MAN. UTD. BEAT ASTON VILLA.

13 WEDNESDAY: FLU' IN SCHOOL
SPREADS. RAIN. NO FOOTBALL.
PLOUGH COMES.

14 THURSDAY: SAT FOR THE 13+.
ARITHMETIC WAS NOT SO BAD. DID WELL
ON ESSAY & ENGLISH. IN THE STAFF
ROOM. WIRELESS.

15 FRIDAY: WATCHED FILM IN SCHOOL.
HAD A GOOD DINNER. MARY CAME DOWN.

16 SATURDAY: WENT UP TO SEE H.B.
FOOTBALL, THEY WON 5-1. WEST HAM 1
EVERTON 0, MAN.UTD. 2 CHELSEA 1,
EXETER WIN AGAIN.

On the 14th March in 1963 I took the 13+ examination in the school staff room alongside another classmate. It gave the opportunity for those pupils who had failed the 11+ but had progressed enough in two years to try again and gain a place at the grammar school. I put in my diary that the Arithmetic was not too bad, and that I did well at English. When the results came through my classmate Jenny had passed and I was considered to be on the borderline.

I decided to stay at the Secondary Modern because my friends were there and I had started to enjoy it. Who knows what might have happened if I had chosen differently and taken another road in life.

My school's attempt to encourage those who wanted to learn was to stream classes into A and B, and sometimes C, grades. In 1963 they even tried dividing pupils into 'Agricultural' and 'Technical', the thinking being that the 'Technical' pupils would gain 'O' Levels and perhaps even 'A' Levels and a university degree, and then go on to progress in the so-called "white heat of technology", one of the defining political slogans of the late sixties. Meanwhile those under the label of 'Agriculture' would be encouraged to leave school early and go into jobs at the local factories or, as most were expected to, go home and work on the family farm. For those from farming families who chose to carry on with further education the decision was often a difficult one, and therefore tinged with some doubt and guilt. This was certainly changing in the increasingly progressive sixties, but it had been much harder in the previous decades.

This was the case with Aunt Phyllis, my father's older sister. She had achieved remarkable progress in her early education but suffered when her own dreams and high expectations were set against her parents' uncertainty about her future. This was a time when women from farming backgrounds rarely attempted further education and were expected to either help at home or to get married. I think these expectations led to a lot of anxiety in her life and perhaps aggravated her periods of mental illness, which would now be recognised as bi-polar.

My great-aunt Dorothy said what most of the older family members probably thought, that Phyllis had "overheated her brain, and that was not good, especially for a woman." My parents would do their best to help her out and have her to stay, but it was often unpredictable, difficult o amusing, such as the time she gave my brother a toilet roll as a Christmas presen

Phyllis was born in 1911, and first went to school in the local village, where she would ride a farm pony there and back every day. She won a scholarship to the Girl's High School in Crediton, were she probably enjoyed some of the happiest days of her life. On leaving there she worked as a pupil-teacher in a primary school, cycling there and back twelve miles a day along some of the most isolated country lanes in Devon.

At the age of eighteen she worked as an unqualified teacher at the Church school in Holsworthy. Then, despite her parents opposition, she went to teacher training college at Loughborough to gain a full Teaching Certificate.

Phyllis Keen in 1933.

During the war she served with the ATS (above), and after some short-lived teaching appointments had a varied life including starting to write a book on village history, volunteering for St John Ambulance, and being a life-model at Exeter Art College. Her Christian faith stayed strong, but her later life went through many ups and downs. Periods of high energy were followed by deep lows, as hinted at in one of her poems:

"It isn't always the bad that go mad,
Some's mad and stay mad, some's bad and
stay bad.
That's sad, to stay either mad or bad.
But some bad go mad, and some mad go bad,
Though they don't stay bad or mad or sad.
They're glad!

The bad's glad because they're not mad,
The mad's glad because they're not bad.
They're glad they're not always bad or mad,
They'd be sad if the bad were always bad,
And if the mad were always mad,
That's bad!

But I am glad that I'm a bit mad,
Between you and me, I'm a little bit bad.
But I'd be sad if I was very bad
And I'd be very mad if I was proper bad".

⬛e was able to borrow forty pounds from ⬛e local education authority, promising to ⬛y them back when qualified. At the end ⬛the course she gained one of the ⬛ghest exam results in the south-west, ⬛d the Professor of Education at the time ⬛ote to her parents to ask them to ⬛nsider allowing her to study for another ⬛elve months. As she wrote in her diary ⬛r parents "considered it for a full two ⬛nutes". They thought about the effect ⬛the household of her not earning for ⬛other year, and suggested that if she ⬛dn't started work at twenty-one she ⬛uld never want to work again. Despite ⬛s she started work as a teacher in ⬛ehampton and within two years had ⬛d back the forty pounds.

Phyllis Mary Keen died in a residential care home in Chudleigh Knighton, Devon on the 17th of March 1987.

She has left us many pages of poetry, stories, letters, postcards and diaries, including her amusing recollections of an early Exeter city twinning visit to Rennes in France in the 1960s.

I found this poem among the many papers she left behind:

"When I was but a girl, and pure,
I dreamt all day how it would be
When I was grown, and I was sure
The future promised fair for me.

That I should climb the scales of fame
And reach the heights of joy and wealth,
That everyone would know my name
And I'd enjoy both love and health.

It did not come to me to pray
That these good things I might achieve
I knew not then that these things may
Be dearly won, I dreamt to receive.

But now I come, 'most past halfway
The allotted span, and I have known
Ill-health, misfortune, giving way,
And other ills, since I have grown.

My dreams have altered with the years,
And now it's peace, the most I crave;
And in its calm, with penitent tears
I move towards a lonely grave.

Yet not a sad stone raise for me,
For there's much that I have had,
Though life's not how I dreamt 'twould be
It has been good, though some was bad.

So in the days that are ahead,
Please God, I'll work, not waste away,
Making and mending things instead
Of dreaming, and follow him and pray".

MARCH 1963

17 SUNDAY: TOOK COLLECTION IN CHURCH. WENT DOWN TO WOODS, ROPE LADDER.

18 MONDAY: MADE A TROLLEY.

19 TUESDAY: BONFIRE. SINGED MY EYELASHES.

20 WEDNESDAY: PLAYED FOOTBALL IN SCHOOL. CAT HAD KITTENS.

21 THURSDAY: NICE DAY. MAN CAME ABOUT BOOKS.

22 FRIDAY: WATCHED A FILM IN SCHOOL ABOUT JULIUS CAESAR. MARY, GRAN, GRANDAD CAME DOWN.

23 SATURDAY: WENT TO SEE H.B. PLAY FOOTBALL, THEY WON 3-2. BURNLEY LOSE, MAN.UTD. LOSE, SPURS DRAW & EXETER WIN AGAIN. OXFORD WIN THE BOAT RACE. DENMARK WIN THE SONG CONTEST.

NOTES FOR MARCH 1963:

10th The 'dykes' in the cover (woodland) were where constant water erosion had created deep ditches in the ground.

11th Ivor Marsh was the headmaster at Chulmleigh secondary school at the time.

21st A door to door salesman persuaded my mother to buy two large home educational books, one on Mathematics and one on English. She hoped it would improve my arithmetic. It didn't.

24th Richard ('Doctor') Beeching published his report on the state of the railways called "The Reshaping of British Railways" which resulted in the closing of many of the smaller branch lines in the network.

30th Pat Buckley was only 19 years old when he rode 'Ayala' to victory in the Grand National.

MARCH 1963

24 SUNDAY: MADE A MAP OF THE WOOD. BEECHING CLOSES MANY RAILWAYS IN HIS PLAN.

25 MONDAY: SAW REST OF FILM IN SCHOOL (GOOD).

26 TUESDAY: COVENTRY BEAT SUNDERLAND. F.A. CUP 5th ROUND, THEY MEET MAN. UTD.

27 WEDNESDAY: TYPHOID FEVER IN BRITAIN. ALL THE VICTIMS WENT TO ZERMATT IN SWITZERLAND FOR THEIR HOLIDAY.

28 THURSDAY: MADE A GOOD HIDE IN THE WOODS. HELPED MUM PAINT WINDOWS. HOLIDAY BECAUSE OF TEACHERS MEETING.

29 FRIDAY: PAINTED STEPS. HOLIDAY. ROGER'S BIRTHDAY.

30 SATURDAY: MAN. UTD. 3-1, LEICESTER 1-0, LIVERPOOL 1-0, NOTTS OR SOUTHAMPTON SEMI-FINALISTS. GRAND NATIONAL WINNER - AYALA RODE BY P. BUCKLEY. AUNT MARY, GRAN, GRANDAD CAME DOWN.

Mrs Margaret 'Molly' Hare, our neighbour who lived at Ward's Cottage during 1963, on her horse (probably 'Cob Nut'.)

MARCH 1963

31 SUNDAY: *PUT CLOCKS FORWARD.*

APRIL 1963

1 MONDAY: *PLAYED A GOOD GAME IN P.E. DON RUTHERFORD IN SCHOOL TEACHING.*

2 TUESDAY: *WENT TO CHITTLEHAMPTON TO SEE THEM PLAY H.B. SCORE H.B. WON 5-2.*

3 WEDNESDAY: *LAST GAME OF FOOTBALL IN SCHOOL, SCORED 2. (BUDGET DAY). ENGLAND BEAT FRANCE 42-4 IN RUGBY. CHULMLEIGH SCHOOL TEAM LOSE 4-2 AT HOLSWORTHY.*

4 THURSDAY: *BROKE UP FROM SCHOOL. PUT WALLPAPER UP IN FRONT ROOM. LADDIE DISAPPEARED.*

5 FRIDAY: *WENT TO BARNSTAPLE, DAD SOLD BULLOCKS. BOUGHT FOOTBALL AND JEANS.*

6 SATURDAY: *DID THE LAMBS. CAME HOME WITH MARY. H.B. BEAT HATHERLEIGH.*

It is the 3rd of April 1963. Budget Day, an the final day of the school term. We play our last games of football on the muddy school field.

The next day, at the very start of my schoc Easter holidays, our sheep dog Laddie disappeared. He was a Welsh border colli a natural expert at rounding up sheep. On most afternoons he would walk patiently beside me as we brought our six cows up the lane for milking. Like all farm dogs in those days, he was never allowed indoors and slept on straw in an outside shed. Even though he did go on to kill my pet guinea pig we were always close, as boys are with dogs. He was a friend, but alway a working dog, not a pet.

However on one occasion he was more than that. We had to move the sheep fro fields on one side of the yard to the othe For some reason I was on my own. A floc of one hundred sheep came tumbling at full speed into the steep yard. Then I noticed the gate had been left open. Dow the slope they ran and straight out throu the open gate. I watched as they charged down the lane, out on to the road, and o of sight. Laddie caught my eye, and I shouted to him to bring them back, and raced off.

I knew it was a vain hope. His pursuit might make things worse: it could make the sheep run faster, up the road, into neighbours' gardens, into the village or i front of a car. The road was very narrow. High banked hedges, thick with primrose squeezed into the road, and there was nowhere to pass. Minutes went by that seemed like hours, and then came the wonderful sight of a flock of sheep come

...ddie outside the front door.

...harging towards me, and into the yard, ...llowed by an exhausted, gasping dog.

...slammed the gate shut, fell to my knees, ...nd gave Laddie a big hug. Our secret. ...o this day I cannot work out how he did it. ...nyway, now I had to start those Easter ...olidays without him around. He had ...andered off before, but not for longer ...an a day.

...ter in the week we went to Exeter and in ...ornish's shop bought a new school ...niform, and afterwards I went to stay at ...y grandparents. A couple of days later ...y aunt drove me home and we arrived ...ck to find Laddie sitting in the yard.

...e had been away exactly seven days, ...riving back under the light of a full ...oon. He was a little thinner and had a ...ry sore neck, but otherwise much the ...me. Like us, Laddie had just come ...rough the hard and bitter winter of ...63. Now the fields had finally thawed ...t, the birds were singing, and Spring was ...the air.

APRIL 1963

7 SUNDAY: WENT OVER TO THE SMALLACOMBES.

8 MONDAY: WENT TO EXETER, BOUGHT SCHOOL UNIFORM. SAW A FILM. MET PHYLLIS AND NINNY. SOUTHAMPTON BEAT NOTTS FOREST AND MAN. UTD. IN THE SEMI-FINAL.

9 TUESDAY: SMALLACOMBES CAME OVER WITH LEO COVEY. PLAYED FOOTBALL AND WATCHED TV.

10 WEDNESDAY: LADDIE CAME BACK, WITH BAD NECK. CAME HOME TO WITHERHILL, PLAYED FOOTBALL, CLEANED OUT TANK, ROGER BREAKS UP FROM SCHOOL.

11 THURSDAY: GRASS SALE AT SNAPE

12 FRIDAY: DID NOT GO TO BARNSTAPLE. CUT THE LAWN. EXETER, PLYMOUTH AND BURNLEY WIN.

13 SATURDAY: HARE HUNTING, ROSE A HARE. CHANNEL CROSSING IN HOT AIR BALLOON. STUDENTS MARCH. BURNLEY LOSE 7-2, SPURS LOSE, MAN.UTD. LOSE, EXETER DREW.

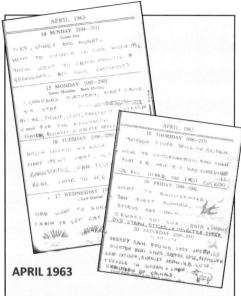

APRIL 1963

14 SUNDAY: WET, WINDY AND MUDDY.
WENT TO CHURCH IN THE MORNING THEN
WENT TO CROCKERNWELL AND
GREENLEAS. ATE SOME EASTER EGGS.

15 MONDAY: GRANDAD'S BIRTHDAY,
OLIVE, PHILIP, GEOFF, MARGARET AND
STEPHEN CAME FOR THE AFTERNOON.
PLAYED BILLIARDS AND WALKED AROUND,
WENT SHOOTING.

16 TUESDAY: WE WENT TO BARNSTAPLE,
CAR TESTED. RENE CAME TO SEE US.

17 WEDNESDAY: DAD WENT TO
BARNSTAPLE BY TRAIN TO GET CAR.

18 THURSDAY: TYPHOID FEVER STILL IN
BRITAIN. WENT TO CHITTLEHAMPTON,
PLAYED HB, WON 5-1, DAD HURT LEG.
WE ALL HEARD THE FIRST CUCKOO.

19 FRIDAY: WENT TO BARNSTAPLE. SAW
FIRST SWALLOW. STICKS ARE SAWN. DID
STRAW, STICKS, AND INJECTED SHEEP.

20 SATURDAY: HEAVY RAIN. FOUND LOST
SHEEP. TROUBLE IN JORDAN AND LAOS.
EXECUTION OF GRIMAU,

It is Easter Monday in 1963, coming afte
a wet, windy and muddy weekend, a
Sunday of church and Easter eggs.
We are walking across the fields with my
father's first cousin Olive and her family;
her husband Philip Uglow, a deputy
headmaster at the local grammar school,
their son Steve, two years older than me
and a pupil at the same school, and their
daughter Margaret, a trainee journalist,
with her new husband Geoff Smith.
As townsfolk Philip and Geoff had
welcomed the opportunity of a walk in th
open countryside to do a spot of shootin
and the chance, however remote, of
bagging a pigeon or two.

The Uglows visiting Witherhill in 1958.

A gun was part of the furniture then,
always at the ready to deal with the foxe
looking to kill chickens, and sometimes t
shoot a pigeon, pheasant or a rabbit for
food. It could lie on the top of a cupboar
with the box of cartridges near at hand,
as in many old farmhouses, it might han
on two nails above the fireplace.
Geoff aimed his gun at some crows in th
distance but they were too far away.

Philip puffed on his pipe and chatted to my father. The hedgerows were silent, with no rabbits or partridges, and the pigeons were away for the day. Steve carried his air-rifle for us to shoot at sparrows or tin cans in the yard, but under the blustery sky we called it a day and went indoors to play billiards.

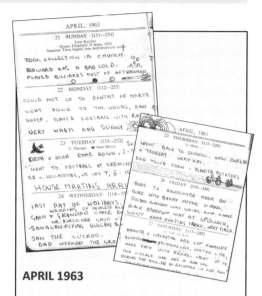

eve and his sisters Margaret and Helen nd I share the same great-grandmother, annah Newcombe (above), by all counts an influential character, who was arried to our great-grandfather Samuel gers. After school Steve attended niversities in England and the USA, and came a lawyer and teacher. In 1971 he arried Jennifer Crowther, who as Jenny glow became a well-known writer of th and 19th century culture. Her work cludes biographies of Elizabeth Gaskell d William Hogarth.

fore leaving Geoff wrote in my tograph book:
ere we are at Witherhill,
ot no pigeons.
aybe the sights are coming loose,
yway that's my excuse".

APRIL 1963

21 SUNDAY: TOOK COLLECTION IN CHURCH. PLAYED BILLIARDS MOST OF THE AFTERNOON. EDWARD HAS A BAD COLD.

22 MONDAY: COULD NOT GO TO DENTIST OR MARYS. WENT DOWN TO THE WOODS, SAW SHEEP. VERY WARM AND SUNNY.

23 TUESDAY: KEITH AND JOHN CAME DOWN. SUNNY. WENT TO FOOTBALL AT FREMINGTON, HOUSE MARTINS ARRIVE.

24 WEDNESDAY: SUNNY. LAST DAY OF HOLIDAYS. MARY, GRAN AND GRANDAD CAME DOWN. WEDDING OF PRINCESS ALEXANDRA AND MR A. OGLIVY. MR PINCOMBE GAVE US A TAME LAMB. SAW A LOW FLYING VULCAN BOMBER. SAW A CUCKOO. DAD WORKED THE GROUND.

25 THURSDAY: WENT BACK TO SCHOOL. NEW BLAZER AND TROUSERS. VERY HOT. DAD TILLED CORN AND PLANTED POTATOES.

26 FRIDAY: RODE TO HOLLACOMBE MOOR ON BIKE WITH BARRY AFTER SCHOOL, DOLTON BEACON WAY GOING. CAME BACK ASHREIGNEY WAY AT TEN O'CLOCK. WENT HARE HUNTING THERE, VERY TIRED.

27 SATURDAY: MADE PATH WITH BRICKS, WENT UP TO THE VILLAGE. NURSES PAY RISE. DID AN EXCHANGE IN 'FOOTBALL MONTHLY'. DAD HAS A BAD LEG.

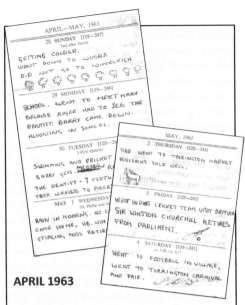

APRIL 1963

28 SUNDAY: GETTING COLDER. WENT DOWN TO THE WOODS. DID NOT GO TO WINKLEIGH.

29 MONDAY: SCHOOL. WENT TO MEET MARY BECAUSE ROGER HAD TO SEE THE DENTIST. BARRY CAME DOWN. RUNNING IN SCHOOL.

30 TUESDAY: SWIMMING AND CRICKET IN SCHOOL. BARRY GETS MIGRAINE. ROGER SAW DENTIST, 7 TEETH OUT, 2 FILLED. TOOK WIRELESS TO PIECES.

MAY 1963

1 WEDNESDAY: RAIN IN MORNING. NO CRICKET. ROGER CAME HOME. H.B. WIN MAN. UTD. WIN. STIRLING MOSS RETIRES.

2 THURSDAY: DAD WENT TO TORRINGTON MARKET. BULLOCKS SOLD WELL.

3 FRIDAY: WEST INDIES CRICKET TEAM VISIT BRITAIN. SIR WINSTON CHURCHILL RETIRES FROM PARLIAMENT.

4 SATURDAY: WENT TO FOOTBALL. WENT TO TORRINGTON CARNIVAL AND FAIR.

NOTES FOR APRIL 1963:

1st Don Rutherford OBE was an England international rugby player and coach.

7th The Smallacombes lived at Natson, Bow.

8th 'Ninny' was my grandmother, my father's mother, who lived at Crockernwell, near Cheriton Bishop.

16th 'Rene' was Rene Vigers, my father's first cousin. Her father was Mark Vigers of Magor i Wales. She married Peter Heartland and emigrated to Australia.

20th Julian Grimau, a Spanish Communist leader, was executed by a firing squad.

23rd John and Keith were the Tuckers from North Road Farm, High Bickington.

23rd House martins made their nests on both sides of the main barn on the farm.

24th Princess Alexandra of Kent, a first cousin the Queen, married Angus Oglivy at Westminster Abbey.

24th The iconic Avro Vulcan bomber was operated by the RAF from 1956 to 1984.

Cheriton Bishop church and the Keens' graves.

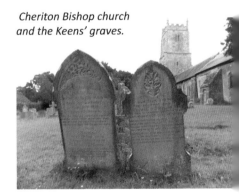

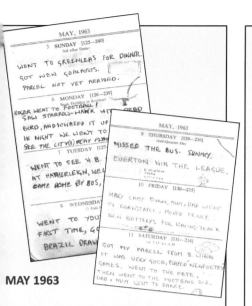

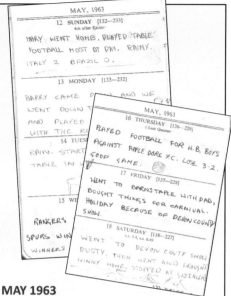

MAY 1963

5 SUNDAY: WENT TO GREENLEAS FOR DINNER. GOT NEW GOALPOSTS. PARCEL NOT YET DELIVERED.

6 MONDAY: SAW SPARROW HAWK WITH DEAD BIRD, I CHASED IT UP THE ROAD. IN NIGHT WENT TO EXETER TO SEE CITY PLAY PLYMOUTH, (1-0) GOOD GAME.

7 TUESDAY: WENT TO SEE H.B. V HATHERLEIGH AT HATHERLEIGH, WE LOST 2-1. CAME HOME BY BUS 10 O'CLOCK.

8 WEDNESDAY: WENT TO YOUTH CLUB FOR FIRST TIME, GOOD FUN. BRAZIL DRAW WITH ENGLAND.

9 THURSDAY: MISSED THE BUS. SUNNY. EVERTON WIN THE LEAGUE.

10 FRIDAY: MARY CAME DOWN. MUM AND DAD WENT BARNSTAPLE. MOVED FENCE. NEW BATTERIES FOR RACING TRACK.

11 SATURDAY: GOT PARCEL FROM B. WINN. VERY GOOD, PLAYED 'NEWFOOTY' GAMES. WENT TO FETE. THEN TO THE FOOTBALL 2-2.
DAD & MUM WENT TO A DANCE.

MAY 1963

12 SUNDAY: MARY WENT HOME. PLAYED TABLE FOOTBALL MOST OF DAY. RAINY. ITALY 2 BRAZIL 0.

13 MONDAY: BARRY CAME DOWN AND WE WENT TO THE WOODS AND PLAYED ON THE STRAW WITH ROPE LADDER.

14 TUESDAY: RAIN. STARTED MAKING SMALL TABLE IN WOODWORK.

15 WEDNESDAY: RANGERS WIN SCOTTISH CUP FINAL. SPURS WIN EUROPEAN CUP WINNERS CUP.

16 THURSDAY: PLAYED FOOTBALL FOR H.B. BOYS v APPLEDORE Y.C. LOSE 3-2, GOOD GAME.

17 FRIDAY: WENT TO BARNSTAPLE WITH DAD. BOUGHT THINGS FOR CARNIVAL. HOLIDAY BECAUSE OF DEVON COUNTY SHOW.

18 SATURDAY: WENT TO DEVON COUNTY SHOW. DUSTY. THEN WENT AND BROUGHT NINNY HOME. STOPPED AT GREENLEAS.

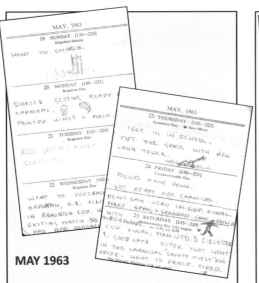

MAY 1963

19 SUNDAY: WENT TO CHURCH.

20 MONDAY: STARTED GETTING READY FOR CARNIVAL. PAINTED WINGS AND MASK.

21 TUESDAY: STILL GETTING READY FOR CARNIVAL.

22 WEDNESDAY: WENT TO FOOTBALL AT BRAUNTON, H.B. PLAYED CHITTLEHAMPTON IN BRAUNTON CUP, WE WON 8-3. EXCITING MATCH, (3-3 10 MINUTES FROM END). HAD A BAD HEADACHE.

23 THURSDAY: FELT ILL IN SCHOOL. CUT GRASS WITH NEW LAWN MOWER.

24 FRIDAY: AUNT PHYLLIS CAME DOWN. GOT READY FOR CARNIVAL.

25 SATURDAY: MARY, GRAN AND GRANDAD CAME DOWN WITH MISS EDWARDS. CUP FINAL: MAN.UTD. 3 LEICESTER 1. DENIS LAW HERO IN CUP FINAL. GOOD GAME.
AFTER THAT WENT IN THE CARNIVAL,"SAFETY FIRST", NO PRIZE. WENT TO DANCE. TIRED.

MAY 1963

26 SUNDAY: CHINGS CAME DOWN. WENT FOR A WALK AROUND FIELDS MRS HARE'S PLACE. CYCLED DOWN TO LITTLE SILVER. SAW TADPOLES IN THE PONDS.

27 MONDAY: EXAMS BEGIN – MATHS, ENGLISH, GEOG. & MUSIC. DID WELL.

28 TUESDAY: DID MATHS, ENGLISH, FRENCH, HISTORY IN EXAMS, ALRIGHT. "SPARKY" COW HAS CALF.

29 WEDNESDAY: NO EXAMS BECAUSE OF SPORTS AT BIDEFORD. HOT.

30 THURSDAY: R.E, T.D. & R.S EXAMS. EDWARD, MUM & I HAVE A BIT OF A COLD POPE VERY ILL.

31 FRIDAY: SCIENCE & BIOLOGY LAST EXAMS. THEN I WENT IN SWIMMING POOL PLAYED CRICKET. VERY HOT.

JUNE 1963

1 SATURDAY: DAD WENT ON CHURCH OUTING TO CORNWALL & PLYMOUTH. HAD TO DO ALL DADS WORK. MARY, GRAN & GRANDAD CAME DOWN TO HELP. NEW CARD ALBUM.

NOTES FOR MAY 1963:

[t] *Stirling Moss, a popular British racing driver, announces his retirement.*

[d] *Sir Winston Churchill, aged 88, announces his retirement from politics due to ill health.*

[th] *'Newfooty' was the original table football game, preceding the better known 'Subbuteo' football game.*

[th] *The Devon County Show was held in 1963 The Whipton Showground in Exeter.*

[th] *Wembley Stadium (fully roofed for the first time) hosted the 1963 Cup Final between Manchester United and Leicester City. Manchester United won 3-1.*

[th] *The Chings were Gordon and Doris Ching Crockernwell, near Cheriton Bishop. Gordon was my fathers first cousin, son of Emma (Keen) and Thomas Ching. Gordon, and later his son Paul, worked as a saddler in Crockernwell.*

Emma Ching (Keen) 1893 - 1971

JUNE 1963

2 SUNDAY: POPE JOHN DIED.

3 MONDAY: WENT TO SPEEDWAY IN EXETER (v NEW CROSS) WON 48-30. WENT TO FILM AT ODEON AFTER. LOT OF TRAFFIC. SUN, RAIN IN AFTERNOON.

4 TUESDAY: PAINTED YARD GATE (RED) ALL MORNING. PLAYED ON TROLLEY.

5 WEDNESDAY: DID NOT GO TO YOUTH CLUB BECAUSE I HAD TO HOE THE POTATOES ON TRACTOR. CLOUDY.

6 THURSDAY: VERY HOT. WENT TO GREENLEAS TO STAY. DAD CUT THE LAWN. IN THE MORNING HOED MANGOLDS ON TRACTOR. NEW JEANS.

7 FRIDAY: WENT TO EXMOUTH BY TRAIN WITH MARY. PLAYED GOLF. SAW THE AQUARIUM, LIFEBOAT, MODEL RAILWAY, TOOK PHOTOGRAPHS, ON BEACH FOR A WHILE. CROWDED. TYPHOID FEVER IN ENGLAND.

8 SATURDAY: CAME HOME WITH MARY AND SMALLACOMBES. THEY STAYED TILL 11 O'CLOCK. PLAYED FOOTBALL AND IN BILLIARD ROOM. HOT.

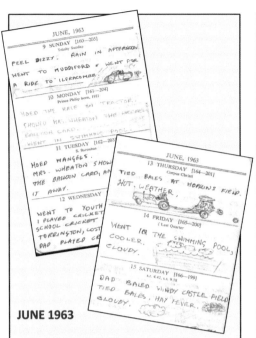

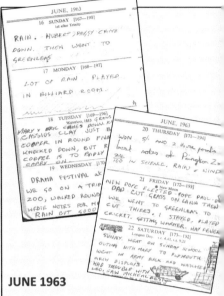

JUNE 1963

9 SUNDAY: FEEL DIZZY. RAIN IN AFTERNOON. WENT TO MUDDIFORD & ON TO ILFRACOMBE.

10 MONDAY: HOED KALE ON TRACTOR. SHOWED MRS WHEATON THE FRENCH BALLOON CARD. WENT IN POOL.

11 TUESDAY: HOED MANGELS. MRS WHEATON SHOWED CLASS THE BALLOON CARD & SENT IT AWAY.

12 WEDNESDAY: WENT TO YOUTH CLUB I PLAYED CRICKET, 2 BOWLED IN 1 OVER. SCHOOL CRICKET TEAM PLAYED TORRINGTON, LOST.
DAD PLAYED CRICKET AT INSTOW.

13 THURSDAY: TIED BALES IN HOPKIN'S FIELD. HOT WEATHER.

14 FRIDAY: WENT IN THE SWIMMING POOL. COOLER, CLOUDY.

15 SATURDAY: DAD BALED WINDY CASTLE FIELD. TIED BALES. HAY FEVER.

JUNE 1963

16 SUNDAY: RAIN. HUBERT & PEGGY CAME DOWN.

17 MONDAY: PLAYED IN BILLIARD ROOM.

18 TUESDAY: MARY & UNCLE ERIC COME DOWN. CASSIUS CLAY JUST BEATS COOPER IN ROUND 5, CLAY KNOCKED DOWN BUT REF SAYS COOPER TOO BADLY BLEEDING TO CARRY ON.

19 WEDNESDAY: DRAMA FESTIVAL AT CHULMLEIGH. WE GO ON A TRIP TO PAIGNTON ZOO, WALKED ROUND WITH REDWOOD. WROTE NOTES FOR MR SIMPSON. RAIN BUT GOOD FUN.

20 THURSDAY: WON 5/- FOR BEST NOTES ON PAIGNTON ZOO. RAIN, WIND.

21 FRIDAY: NEW POPE ELECTED- POPE PAUL. DAD CUT LAWN GRASS THEN WENT TO GREENLEAS TO CUT THEIRS.

22 SATURDAY: WENT ON SUNDAY SCHOOL OUTING WITH MARY TO PLYMOUTH. WATCHED ARMY DISPLAYS. HAD TROUBLE WITH LEO. SAW MICHAEL BEST.

It is midsummer, the 18th of June, 1963. In my diary I see it is the day the Battle of Waterloo was fought, in 1815. On that day the Duke of Wellington would have been watching the 73,000 French troops on the opposite hill and considering his chances.

Today is also my grandmother's birthday, and apart from my father and me the other members of the family are all indoors, topping and tailing gooseberries and having tea. A warm summer breeze is blowing through the house and quietly moving the sticky amber glue strips that hang over the kitchen table to catch flies.

I'm walking to the centre of a field above the farm, carrying the rat trap, a wire cage with five large rats inside, a rolling brown ball of sinew and tail. Running beside me is a very excited terrier, a prime rat-catcher. He is a Jack Russell, one of the breed named the famous rector of Swimbridge in North Devon. (Parson Jack was a typical larger-than-life Victorian country vicar, an energetic huntsman and sportsman who was responsible for the breed of dog that bore his name, specially bred to dig out any foxes that had "gone to ground". It was said that his sermons were very short by Victorian standards as his horse was always ready saddled-up and waiting outside the church for him).

Not much rat poison was used on the farm in the 1960s, and to control the rat population we relied on the owls that lived in the top barn, the numerous cats and their feral friends that came and went, the terrier if he was lucky, and the wire cage traps from which there was no escape. It was the time of year when the cage traps in the barns were often occupied when we went to inspect them in the mornings.

The usual disposal was to drop the cage, attached to a cord, into the black water of the old horse-trough at the top of the yard, but as there was no-one to see what I was doing I thought I'd give the rats a sporting chance.

The dog waited, barking wildly. Swallows and house martins swooped and looped around us catching insects, and two buzzards lazily circled high above us. We were in a five acre field, recently cut for hay. I guessed a good thirty yards to the farmyard gate, perhaps twenty yards to the safety of the nearest hedge. The rats chewed at the metal bars. What were their chances? Perhaps they were one family?

Rats are one of the most intelligent of all creatures. Did they comprehend the situation? Could they calculate the distance to run? Would they choose the option of running in one way or the other, a zig-zag or a direct line, in a group or in different directions. Could they outrun the killing-dog? Was there hope in those small black eyes? Rats are great survivors, if there *is* a way they'll find it, any small gap, any chance of food, any fight to the death. Five against one. What chance?

Harvest time at my grandparents' farm, Appledore Farm, Bow in the 1930s.

I hold the dog collar, watching my fingers. I carefully open the cage door. Five rats fall into the grass. One is too slow , but four race away. I release the straining collar.

The terrier's jaws snap: one down. Another quick shake, and a neck breaks in a second. The dog twists and turns, snaps at a third, gives a shake of the jaw, and another is gone. The dog spots the last two, a last chance dash to the hedge, too late for one. One is gone, however, I think one made it. I think one took the chance. I think one got away.

After tea and cakes we watched the black and white television on the kitchen sideboard. It was the big fight: Henry Cooper against the up-and-coming Cassius Clay. Our hero Henry, cockney nice-guy against the young loud-mouth American. What chance? Cooper knocks Clay down, but by round five the referee has to stop the fight. Cooper is bleeding heavily and cannot carry on. No chance.

The next day is a school trip to Paignton Zoo. We walk around in the continuous drizzle, taking notes. I watch a leopard pacing up and down behind the wire cage of its enclosure. Up and down, up and down, up and down all day. Is there a way out, please? A way back to the homeland, the hot African sky, racing the gazelle? Or just a chance to get to those hills above the zoo, chasing rabbits through the gorse and heather, dripping wet and happy in the Dartmoor rain. Was there a chance? Was there any hope in those yellow eyes?

That afternoon we go to my grandparents and I stay on for the weekend. A warm mid-summer night, and in the morning the start of the longest day of the year.

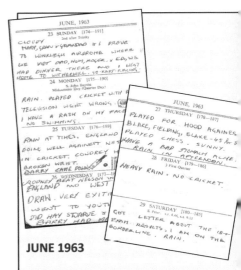

JUNE 1963

23 SUNDAY: CLOUDY. MARY, GRAN AND GRANDAD DROVE TO WINKLEIGH AERODROME TO MEET MUM, DAD, ROGER & ED. HAD DINNER THERE. WENT GO-KARTING, WENT HOME.

24 MONDAY: RAIN. PLAYED CRICKET. TELEVISION WENT WRONG. HAVE A RASH ON MY FACE. NO SWIMMING.

25 TUESDAY: RAIN AT TIMES. ENGLAND DOING WELL AGAINST WEST INDIES. COWDREY HAS A BROKEN WRIST. BARRY CAME DOWN.

26 WEDNESDAY: RODNEY BEAT NELSON IN CRICKET. ENGLAND & WEST INDIES DRAW. VERY EXCITING. WENT TO YOUTH CLUB. DID HAY SWARF AND DUG WEEDS. BARRY HAS MIGRAINE.

27 THURSDAY: PLAYED FOR HOOD v BLAKE, FIELDING. BLAKE 45 FOR 5. PLAYED CHESS. HAVE A BAD STOMACH ACHE. RAIN IN AFTERNOON.

28 FRIDAY: HEAVY RAIN. NO CRICKET.

29 SATURDAY: GOT LETTER ABOUT THE 13+ EXAM RESULTS, I AM ON THE BORDERLINE. RAIN.

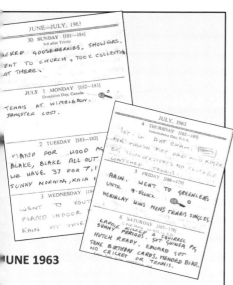

JUNE 1963

30 SUNDAY: PICKED GOOSEBERRIES, SHOWERS. WENT TO CHURCH, TOOK COLLECTION, LOT THERE.

JULY 1963

. MONDAY: TENNIS AT WIMBLEDON. SANGSTER LOST.

. TUESDAY: PLAYED FOR HOOD v BLAKE, BLAKE ALL OUT FOR 45. US 37 FOR 7. I'M TILL IN. SUNNY, RAIN IN AFTERNOON.

WEDNESDAY: WENT TO YOUTH CLUB. LAYED INDOOR GAMES. RAIN.

THURSDAY: FIRST IN ART EXAM. MR MARSH MET DAD AND ROGER. BIG THUNDERSTORM. NO CRICKET. WATCHED ENNIS.

FRIDAY: RAIN. WENT TO GREENLEAS. NTIL 9 O'CLOCK. McKINLAY WINS MEN'S ENNIS SINGLES.

SATURDAY: LADDIE KILLED A SQUIRREL. UNNY PERIODS. GOT GUINEA PIG HUTCH EADY. EDWARD GOT SOME BIRTHDAY ARDS. MENDED BIKE. O CRICKET OR TENNIS.

NOTES FOR JUNE 1963:

2ⁿᵈ Pope John dies, aged 81 years, of cancer.

3ʳᵈ Exeter Speedway meetings were held at the County Ground.

6ᵗʰ I would drive the tractor along, at minimum speed, between the rows of mangolds (a variety of beet) or sometimes potatoes while my father controlled the hoe behind. At the end of each row I had to stop while my father unhitched the hoe, turned the tractor around and we'd start again. This job was once done by Jim Patt and his working cart horse Daisy.

10ᵗʰ Mrs Wheaton was our French teacher, who lived at the Garage near Eggesford on the A377 road. I had found a burst balloon in one of our fields that had blown over from France with a note in French on it. We did write a reply but never heard anything back.

16ᵗʰ Hubert was Hubert Vigers, my father's first cousin. He lived at Venny Tedburn, near Crediton, with his wife Peggy and daughter Ruth.

18ᵗʰ The boxer Cassius Clay later changes his name to Muhammad Ali.

19ᵗʰ 'Redwood' was Robert Redwood of Chulmleigh. His father was a butcher in the town. Mr Simpson was our art teacher.

22ⁿᵈ Michael Best was a cousin from Bow, son of Roy and Gladys (Pickard) Best.

23ʳᵈ Winkleigh Aerodrome is a disused World War Two airfield. Where I, and a lot of local people, first started to learn to drive.

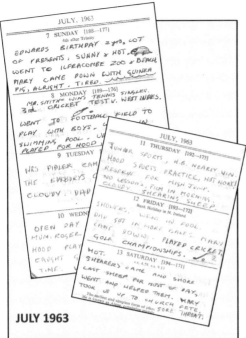

JULY 1963

7 SUNDAY: EDWARD'S BIRTHDAY, 2 YRS.
LOT OF PRESENTS. SUNNY & HOT. WENT
TO ILFRACOMBE BEACH & ZOO. MARY
CAME DOWN WITH GUINEA PIG,

8 MONDAY: THIRD TEST V WEST INDIES.
WENT TO FOOTBALL FIELD TO PLAY WITH
BOYS. WENT IN POOL. PLAYED FOR HOOD,
BEAT BLAKE.

9 TUESDAY: MRS PIDLER CAME DOWN, &
THE BURBERRYS CAME TO VISIT US.
CLOUDY. DAD BROUGHT IN BALES.

10 WEDNESDAY: OPEN DAY IN SCHOOL.
DAD, MUM, ROGER, MARY & ED. CAME IN.
CAUGHT GUINEA PIG FIRST TIME.

11 THURSDAY: JUNIOR SPORTS. NO
LESSONS. FILM IN MORNING. SHEARING
SHEEP.

12 FRIDAY: SHOWERS. WENT IN POOL. DAD
GOT IN MORE BALES. MARY CAME DOWN.
PLAYED CRICKET.

13 SATURDAY: HOT. SHEARERS CAME FOR
MOST OF DAY. WENT AND HELPED THEM.
MARY TOOK US UP TO CHURCH FETE.
SORE THROAT.

It is early summer in 1963. I am lying in the centre of a field, in clover-rich green grass which is alive with busy ladybirds and grasshoppers. I watch the trail of a jet as it cuts a white line across the clear blue sky. The hedgerows that enclose the square field shimmer with butterflies feeding on flowers and wild honeysuckle. I watch a skylark rising vertically up into the warm air. As it gets higher it starts to sing, rich liquid notes that fill the sky. The lark ascending, climbing its way to heaven.

Then at a certain height and almost invisible to the eye, it suddenly stops singing and slowly drops down, back down into the field. Then twisting and turning through the grass it returns to the hidden nest. This tactic makes the nest almost impossible   to find, and something I'd always hoped I'd manage one day.
The collecting of birds eggs was made unlawful, with some exceptions, in 1954, but in the countryside it was still carried on as a hobby for many years.

For me and my school friends it went alongside our collecting of stamps or tea cards. When we found a nest a single egg would be removed, with care not to touch the others. It was taken home and a pinhole would be made at each end and the yolk and white blown out into a cup. (If they were left inside, the egg would slowly rot). It would be put on a tray of sawdust, labelled, and placed with others in neat rows of various colours and sizes. They were our treasures, displayed like diamonds and rubies, our prizes after days of hunting and searching. As the years passed however, they were put away at the back of a cupboard, and forgotten.

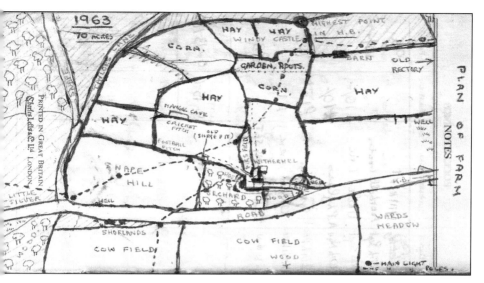

On one of the first pages of the diary I drew a plan of the farm as it was in 1963. Bill Pidler, the previous owner, had a map with field names on, now lost. The mains electric lines are shown.

ery part of the farm had its own special bitat and for every kind of bird its own ecial piece of landscape. In the valley, here a small stream spluttered its way rough the woodland a kingfisher might seen, and I might spot a woodpecker ecking the rough bark of the oak trees.

ar the farmyard was the nest of a wren, gically woven in moss between the ones by the well. In the farmyard itself e returning house martins had built their mes of mud under the eaves of the ed, competing with noisy sparrows for ace. On the top of a supporting post in e open barn a spotted flycatcher fed her ung, safe from rats and farmyard cats.

ould go through a gate to a piece of land ce called the cherry orchard. In there a oked old holly tree, tangled in ivy, held arge magpie's nest. Then upwards into high, open fields with flocks of rooks, wings, and the hovering kestrel.

I watched the skylark drop into the deep grass. Then I slowly rose up, keeping my eyes glued to the landing spot. Reaching it I estimated a five yard diameter circle, and walked carefully around it, lifting any folded grass, not disturbing anything. Ten minutes passed and I found nothing. Too clever for us, the master of camouflage.

The skylark population has fallen by more than 50% since those days, it is simply a loss of habitat caused by the changes in farming practice with the demand for cheaper food, and the ever-growing population that needs more houses, and more land to build them on. I trudged back down to the farmhouse and our tea, and I resigned myself to never finding a skylark's nest.

Now I wonder if my grandchildren and their children will resign themselves to never seeing a skylark, or hearing its song, as it climbs its way to heaven.

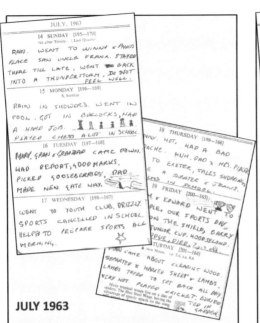

JULY 1963

14 SUNDAY: RAIN. WENT TO NINNY & PHYLLIS. SAW UNCLE FRANK. STAYED THERE 'TIL LATE. WENT BACK INTO A THUNDERSTORM. DO NOT FEEL WELL.

15 MONDAY: RAIN IN SHOWERS. WENT IN POOL. GOT IN BULLOCKS.

16 TUESDAY: SCHOOL REPORT, GOOD MARKS. PICKED GOOSEBERRIES. DAD MADE A NEW GATEWAY.

17 WEDNESDAY: WENT TO YOUTH CLUB. SPORTS CANCELLED IN SCHOOL. HELPED TO PREPARE SPORTS ALL MORNING.

18 THURSDAY: HOT. HAD A BAD HEADACHE. MUM, DAD & MRS PIDLER WENT TO EXETER, SALES SHOPPING. GOT ME A SWEATER & JEANS. SAW FILMS IN SCHOOL.

19 FRIDAY: DAD, MUM & EDWARD WENT TO BARNSTAPLE. SPORTS DAY IN SCHOOL. BLAKE WON SHIELD. TED, OUR BUDGIE DIED, 7 YEARS OLD.

20 SATURDAY: MAN CAME ABOUT CLEARING WOOD. SEPARATED AND MARKED SHEEP AND LAMBS. LAMBS TRIED TO GET BACK ALL DAY. BURIED TED IN GARDEN.

JULY 1963

21 SUNDAY: WENT TO CHURCH. TOOK EDWARD FOR A WALK IN WOODS. HAD OUR HAIR CUT. NOT FEELING WELL.

22 MONDAY: DAD HAS A BAD EYE. BALING HAY. GUINEA PIG GETTING TAMER. TIED BALES. WENT IN POOL.

23 TUESDAY: PLAYED CRICKET FOR HOOD v NELSON. WE WIN CRICKET CUP. TIED BALES. SONNY LISTON BEATS PATTERSON IN 2 MINUTES, CASSIUS IS ANGRY!

24 WEDNESDAY: PLAYED CRICKET FOR 2A v 2B. I SCORE MOST RUNS (13). WENT TO YOUTH CLUB. CHULMLEIGH FAIR WEEK. PRIZE DAY IN SCHOOL.

25 THURSDAY: LAST DAY OF TERM. PLAYED CRICKET. VERY HOT. END OF TERM SERVICE. TOOK IN BALES.

26 FRIDAY: DID NOT GO BARNSTAPLE. PAINTED CHAIRS & HELPED LOAD BALES ON TRAILER. TEST MATCH.

27 SATURDAY: WENT ON SUNDAY SCHOOL OUTING TO TEIGNMOUTH WITH BARRY. 2 HOUR MACKEREL FISHING, CAUGHT A BIG MACKEREL. WENT IN ROWING & MOTOR BOATS. GOOD FUN. SUNNY. WENT ON PIER.

On St. Swithin's Day in 1963 I stood on the concrete edge of our new school swimming pool with a line of other 13-year-old boys of my class. This was one of our first times in the pool, and one of the first days anyone had used it. It was the pride and joy of the school staff who for more than a year, with the help of senior boys and volunteers, had dug, tiled and concreted most of the structure.

We were nervous.

Swimwear was not our usual style of dress, and although the sun was shining, it felt cool on that July day. We trembled in anticipation looking down into that three - four feet of sparkling, shimmering and mysterious blue. The teacher in charge was Mr Davies, a small quick-tempered Welshman who also taught PE and history. football matches he would like to show of his skills to us and hated to be beaten.

Now he marched up and down behind us barking orders. There was no teacher in the pool to guide or help us. We were just instructed to jump into the water as he hit on the back, one by one.

my side was Walter, a boy from the next village. He was pale, shivering and overweight in a time when being overweight was unusual for a schoolboy. suffered from a stammer and wore glasses which he had now removed. He was not unpopular, not bullied, just maybe little more grown-up than the rest of us.

stared into the pool. We were country boys, brought up in windswept villages on ancient ridgeway tracks, and from farms in remote wooded valleys. Our only acquaintance with water was the weekly bath, and perhaps a rare visit to the seaside to paddle at the water's edge or in the rock pools. Those who were lucky had parents who could swim or knew of friends or family with a pool. Of course in the streams and rivers that meandered through the oak woods and cow meadows we would play in water, building dams to catch minnows and sticklebacks as dragonflies hovered around us, but we always heeded the warning to avoid the dark pools, the hidden depths that lay in wait for the unwary or the adventurous.

Now everyone was supposed to jump into the water in turn. Two of us already had, and Walter was next. He looked into the moving surface below. He had seen the swimmers on the television, the great Olympians like Anita Lonsbrough, slipping easily into the water, but when the slap hit his back, in his panic and muddled vision, he fell forward into a half-dive, a spectacular belly-flop.

I then jumped in. He floundered, went under again, then came back up again splashing and gulping at the gagging blue, chlorine water, his legs heavy and unmoving below him. He grabbed me and I managed to steady him. Spluttering and shaking he sat on the pool side for the rest of the lesson and would never go near the swimming pool again.

Walter left school a year before me but in his final term he made it into the school cricket team. For many of us the school cricket season was an all-too-short sports period to enjoy before the summer holidays. Those who had endured long, wet wintry days watching or attempting to play football or rugby now had a chance to shine. Walter did, he had a natural talent as a spin bowler, inspired by his cricketing heroes like Fred Trueman and Fred Titmus. On the school playing fields, the air rich with the smell of new mown grass, he would send the spinning ball towards the wicket. Hitting the ground, it would go in one of several directions, and as the school wicket-keeper I would kneel like England's keeper Jim Parks, trying to guess the direction of the ball as it passed the batsman, passed the stumps, and me.

Walter was also chosen for a part in the end-of-term school play: a comic role in a Shakespeare play suited him down to the ground. He raised his voice, the stutter gone, the cardboard sword waved in triumph and the entire audience reduced to tears of laughter. That term was over too soon, and the dreams were packed away with the schoolbooks. Walter left school, aged fifteen, to work with his father on their market garden.

In the school holidays on a Friday I would go into Barnstaple with my parents, like many families, to visit the market. Walter would be there every week, standing

behind a stall in the busy pannier market with his mother and father, selling their eggs, home-grown fruit, and vegetables.

In the late sixties I started work in the town and would often drop by to see Walter on a Friday lunchtime. Even then the old market was beginning to change, stalls selling cheap clothes were moving i as the stalls that sold farm produce move out. In those days I had become distracte by music and mini-skirts but Walter alway remained the same in his glasses and lon grey coat dispensing words of wisdom or the fast-changing world around him, as h had for years past, and would do so for many long years to come.

For most of us the swimming pool was built far too late, without a good coach o a swimming instructor to guide us along not many of us took it any further.

Yet the fear of deep water, of being out c our depth, would always be with us.

On that St Swithin's Day in 1963 the rain came in silently, late in the afternoon, or our routine bus journey home.

The opening of the Chulmleigh School swimming pool in 1962.

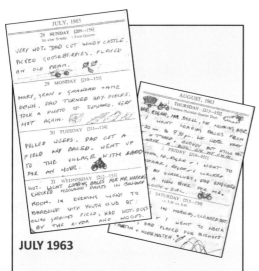

JULY 1963

28 SUNDAY: VERY HOT. DAD CUT WINDY CASTLE. PICKED GOOSEBERRIES. PLAYED WITH OLD PRAM.

29 MONDAY: MARY, GRAN & GRANDAD CAME DOWN. DAD TURNED HAY FIELD. TOOK PHOTO OF EDWARD. HOT AGAIN.

30 TUESDAY: PULLED WEEDS. DAD CUT FIELD AND BALED. WENT TO VILLAGE WITH BARRY FOR AN HOUR.

31 WEDNESDAY: LOADING BALES FOR MR HOPKINS. CHECKED MECCANO PARTS. IN BILLIARD ROOM. IN EVENING WENT TO BARBECUE AT CLIVE GOODINGS FIELD. HAD HOT DOGS BY THE RIVER AND WOODS.

AUGUST 1963

1 THURSDAY: DAD, ROGER, MR SNELL, MR HOPKINS, DAVE & I WENT LOADING BALES FROM 10.30am TO 9.30pm. CLOUDY BUT STILL HOT. HAVE BOIL ON MY CHIN.

2 FRIDAY: WE ALL WENT TO BARNSTAPLE. DAD ENQUIRED ABOUT A NEW BIKE FOR ME. VERY CLOUDY AND DULL.

3 SATURDAY: RAIN & FOG. WE WENT TO NORTH MOLTON, DAD PLAYED FOR BISHOP'S TAWTON v NORTH MOLTON.

NOTES FOR JULY 1963:

1st Devon born Mike Sangster was Britain's number one tennis player in the 1960s.

7th Ilfracombe Zoo operated from 1949 to 1973. Owned by Charles Trevisick.

9th Mrs Pidler was the wife of Bill Pidler, the previous owners of the farm. Wing Commander Burberry and his wife were former neighbours at Shoplands.

13th The sheep shearers were the Coates brothers from Muddiford, a small village just north of Barnstaple. My father would meet them at The Muddiford Inn to arrange the shearing dates.

16th My father made a new gateway, cut through the hedge from the field at Windy Castle to the field adjoining Beechwood.

19th Sports Day. The school houses were Blake, Rodney, Nelson and Hood.

23rd Sonny Liston beats Floyd Patterson.

Aunt Mary with Gran and Grandad Pickard outside 'Greenleas' in the early 1960s.

"**J**ournal, missus!" old Dave Pickard would shout at my mother every Thursday morning when I was growing up, as he threw the *North Devon Journal* newspaper onto the stone floor of our hallway. The *Journal* was required reading for all our news in those days. (I even got hold of a copy when I was working years later in London, and feeling homesick). Dave would then carry on down the country road to Deepy Lane which, as the name suggests, drops into a deep wooded valley, and would visit a small paddock where he kept some goats for milking.

Old Dave had always fascinated me, from the time when my parents first moved to the farm in the fifties, (when he'd call me "Nipper") to the mid-sixties and my leaving school. Although I've long forgotten the exact features of his stubbly face, I have not forgotten him. He was one of those out-of-the-ordinary characters, living not quite as expected, perhaps eccentric, or just different. Many existed in the countryside in those days, untouched and able to live as they liked without judgement and interference from local authorities, whereas in the towns they would be much more visible. Another two were the couple who lived at the bottom of 'Deepy' Lane in a caravan. They had been bombed out in the war and now refused to live in a house. He would sit on a bicycle with no chain, a hessian sack over his head, while his wife wheeled him along the road. Said to be very intelligent, he compiled crosswords for national newspapers.

As a child you are intrigued by such strong characters and you never forget them. Another was a very elderly lady I was once introduced to at Clannaborough rectory, near Bow. Almost blind, she wore dark glasses and was one hundred years old. Although it had been many years since she had lost her husband, she still wore black. He had been a farmer who kept a pack of otter hounds, the big dogs that hunted the Taw Valley. She reached out a bony white hand and felt the sheriff's badge I was wearing on my cowboy outfit. At only five years old I could not appreciate that she had grown up in the age of real cowboys, before our world of cars and air travel. Like Dave Pickard she knew stories that would go with her passing, stories I was then too young to care about.

Great-grandmother Pickard with me at 'Greenleas', Bow, in May 1950.
Born Mary Reed at East Arson, Winkleigh in 1861. She married William Pickard in 1884. She died in 1954 at Exmouth and is buried in Bow Congregational churchyard.

Dave Pickard lived all his life in North Devon, first working as a waggoner with cart-horses and helping with jobs on local farms. He dressed in the style of all farm workers of his generation, thick, heavy boots, sometimes with leather leggings, trousers held up by belt and braces, and a waistcoat over a pale shirt. He was never without a sturdy flat cap and always in his mouth, under a thick moustache, a battered old pipe struggled to stay alight in all weathers. With his wife Elizabeth he lived in a small, thatched cottage in the village, and when she died he looked after himself as best he could. Dave helped on the farm, mainly at harvest time.

Grandad Pickard and Edward, June 1963.

The Pickards (Pickard was also my mother's family name) had originated from Picardy in north-west France, and were supposedly named after the pike-staffs their soldiers used to carry with them into battle.

Those who emigrated to this country mostly settled in Yorkshire, but also around the busy harbour town of Bideford in North Devon. Many Pickards would leave from this port in the 1800s along with other families to settle in Canada.

Dave would return to his ancestral homeland in France when he was called up to fight in the First World War, in the mud and blood of Ypres. Sitting at the farmhouse kitchen table, after my mother had made tea for us all, he recalled how young officers would drink deeply from their hip-flasks before going over the top.

One day late in July in 1963 I remember Dave helping my father finish the hay harvest with my brother, Mr Hopkins, and Peter Snell from the village and me. We worked from about nine in the morning, after my father had milked the cows, until late into the night, as rain was predicted for the next day.

As usual, Dave was perched on the trailer, pipe in mouth, and the others pitch-forked the small bales up to him to lift up by the cords and lay in compact rows. Then my father would drive the tractor, a small blue Fordson Dexta, to the next stack of bales we'd gathered up. When the trailer was full a long rope was thrown over the bales and tied in tightly to hold the load as it was driven down into the farmyard. Laddie, our collie, ran alongside and swallows swept low over the new-cut grass. Load after load was brought down to go into the tallet above the stables, or into the barns, disturbing the sparrows and house martins nesting in the eaves. Hot, with sore hands, covered in dust and pestered by flies we'd watch as the field slowly emptied of bales through the long day, only broken up by my mother and aunt bringing tea, orange-squash, cake and sandwiches up to the field.

I could then sit on a pile of bales and, as it was the highest point in the parish, I could look to Dartmoor in the south, up the river valley to Barnstaple, to the hills of Exmoor to the north, and all around me at a patchwork pattern of fields in the haze of summer. I'd watch Dave briefly remove his cap and wipe the sweat and dust away, then light his pipe again and move back to work. My mother and baby brother would pick gooseberries from the hedges that were alive with bees and butterflies.

At last the final load, with Dave sitting on top, would make its way home, wheels creaking down the stone track into the shadows of the farmyard for the last time and the summer night would come alive with moths, flying beetles, and bats.

Walking to the village I would often meet Dave going on down to feed his goats. I don't remember anything that he said in those distant days but I can still see him standing in the lane, the high hedges full of ferns, wild strawberries, honeysuckle and dog rose, or sitting in the farm kitchen where on the side-board the flickering images on our black and white television told us of an outside world which was turning upside-down: the strange new world of the space race and Vietnam, Bob Dylan, the Beatles and the Stones.

Dave's small goat paddock has long been consumed by the surrounding woodland, the farm is silent, the hay barns converted to houses. His old cottage is now highly desirable, and his world gone forever.

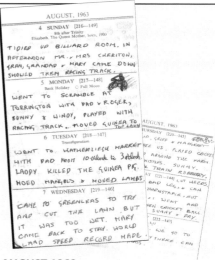

AUGUST 1963

4 SUNDAY: MR & MRS CHERITON VISITED WITH GRAN, GRANDAD AND AUNT MARY.

5 MONDAY: WENT TO A SCRAMBLE AT TORRINGTON. PLAYED WITH RACING TRACK. MOVED GUINEA PIG TO LAWN.

6 TUESDAY: WENT WITH DAD TO HATHERLEIGH MARKET. HOED MANGOLDS AND MOVED LAMBS. LADDIE KILLED THE GUINEA PIG.

7 WEDNESDAY: WENT TO GREENLEAS TO CUT THE LAWN, BUT TOO WET. MARY CAME BACK. WORLD LAND SPEED RECORD BROKEN.

8 THURSDAY: OLIVE, PHILIP, GEOFF & MARGARET CAME TO VISIT. PLAYED CRICKET. CUT THISTLES. BIG TRAIN ROBBERY.

9 FRIDAY: MUM HAS BAD LEG & CAN'T GO TO BARNSTAPLE BUT WE ALL GO. ROGER BOUGHT A CRICKET BALL. PLAYED CRICKET. SUNNY AND DRY.

10 SATURDAY: RAIN, DRIZZLE. WE GO TO GREENLEAS, I STAY. CANNOT CUT GRASS.

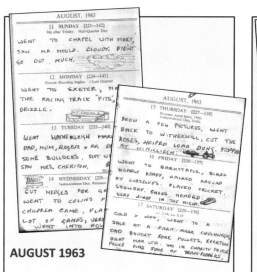

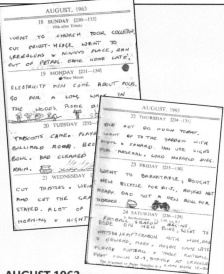

AUGUST 1963

11 SUNDAY: WENT TO CHAPEL WITH AUNT MARY, SAW MR MOULD. CLOUDY. DIDN'T GO OUT MUCH.

12 MONDAY: WENT TO EXETER. MADE RACING TRACK PITS, GOOD. DRIZZLE.

13 TUESDAY: WENT TO HATHERLEIGH MARKET. DAD SOLD SOME BULLOCKS. SAW MRS CHERITON.

14 WEDNESDAY: CUT HEDGES FOR GRANDAD. WENT TO COLIN'S PARTY. 14 CHILDREN CAME. PLAYED A LOT OF GAMES, VERY GOOD FUN. WENT INTO BOW.

15 THURSDAY: DREW A FEW PICTURES. WENT BACK TO WITHERHILL STOPPED AT WINKLEIGH. CUT THE ROSES.
HELPED LOAD DUNG.

16 FRIDAY: WENT TO BARNSTAPLE, BIKES NEARLY READY. WALKED AROUND BY OURSELVES. SHOES MENDED. VERY WINDY IN NIGHT.

17 SATURDAY: COLD & WET. WENT TO A SALE AT A FARM NEAR CHULMLEIGH. DAD BOUGHT SOME PULLETS. EVERTON BEAT MAN. UTD. IN CHARITY SHIELD. POLICE FIND SOME OF TRAIN ROBBERS.

AUGUST 1963

18 SUNDAY: WENT TO CHURCH, TOOK COLLECTION. CUT PRIVET HEDGE. WENT TO GREENLEAS & NINNYS. RAN OUT OF PETROL, CAME HOME LATE.

19 MONDAY: ELECTRICITY MEN COME ABOUT POLES. GO FOR A LONG WALK IN WOODS.

20 TUESDAY: TAPSCOTTS CAME. BROKE HORACE'S BOWL. DAD CLEANED YARD. HEAVY RAIN.

21 WEDNESDAY: CUT THISTLES. WENT TO GREENLEAS. LOT OF RAIN.

22 THURSDAY: DID NOT DO MUCH.
IAN URE SIGNS FOR ARSENAL.

23 FRIDAY: WENT TO BARNSTAPLE, BOUGHT NEW BICYCLE FOR £11 5s. DAD BOUGHT NEW BOWL FOR HORACE.

24 SATURDAY: FOOTBALL SEASON STARTS. RODE NEW BIKE. WE ALL WENT TO NATSON. PLAYED FOOTBALL & TABLE FOOTBALL., BEAT COLIN 12-1. CAME HOME 12 O'CLOCK.

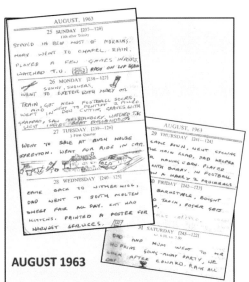

AUGUST 1963

25 SUNDAY: STAYED IN BED MOST OF MORNING. MARY WENT TO CHAPEL.

26 MONDAY: WENT TO EXETER WITH MARY ON TRAIN, GOT NEW FOOTBALL SOCKS, WENT TO DENTIST, 2 FILLED. WENT TO BOW CUTTING GRAVES WITH GRANDAD. SAW MRS STANBURY. WEST INDIES BEAT ENGLAND.

27 TUESDAY: WENT TO SALE AT BUSH HOUSE, SPREYTON, AND A CAR RIDE.

28 WEDNESDAY: CAME BACK TO WITHERHILL. DAD WENT TO SOUTH MOLTON SHEEP FAIR ALL DAY. CAT HAD KITTENS. PAINTED POSTER FOR HARVEST SERVICES.

29 THURSDAY: DAD HELPED MR TUCKER WITH CORN. PLAYED FOOTBALL WITH BARRY. SAW A HARE & 2 SQUIRRELS.

30 FRIDAY: WENT TO BARNSTAPLE. BOUGHT COMICS. ROGER GETS BIKE MENDED. MAINS LIGHT POLES ERECTED.

31 SATURDAY: DAD & MUM WENT TO MR HOPKINS GOING AWAY PARTY, WE LOOK AFTER EDWARD. RAIN ALL DAY.

NOTES FOR AUGUST 1963:

1st Mr Snell was Pete Snell from the village.

2nd The bike shop was in the Newport area of Barnstaple.

4th Henry Cheriton and his wife lived at Clannaborough Rectory, near Bow. For some years they had a railway carriage and signals from the old Barnstaple to Lynton railway line in their garden. It is now in the Railway Museum in York.

5th A "scramble" was another word for moto-cross motorcycle racing.

7th On the 5th Craig Breedlove broke the world land speed record on Bonneville salt flats in the USA, at over 400mph.

8th The Great Train Robbery occurred in Buckinghamshire. £2.6 million was stolen.

12th The racing track was made by Airfix and was similar to Scalextric racing game.

14th Colin was Colin Smallacombe of Natson Farm, Bow.

17th Pullets are young hens under a year old, not yet laying.

22nd Ian Ure was a Scottish international centre-half footballer and signed for £62,500.

26th Our family dentist was Wilfred Selley of Sidwell Street, Exeter.

31st Mr and Mrs Hopkins lived at Nethergrove Farm, High Bickington.

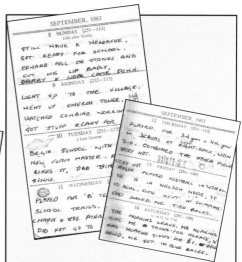

SEPTEMBER 1963

1 SUNDAY: DID NOT DO MUCH. RAIN ALL DAY. PAINTED POSTERS.

2 MONDAY: BIT BETTER WEATHER. BARRY & KEITH CAME DOWN. PLAY IN HAY BARNS & MADE TUNNELS. WENT TO VILLAGE, HAD A HAIR CUT.

3 TUESDAY: BARRY & KEITH CAME DOWN MOST OF DAY. PLAYED IN BARNS HOT & SUNNY.

4 WEDNESDAY: MARY, GRAN AND GRANDAD CAME DOWN, HAVE NOT GOT THEIR NEW CAR. ROGER HAD HAIR CUT. WENT TO YOUTH CLUB.

5 THURSDAY: BARRY DOWN MOST OF DAY. PLAYED IN HAY. MADE & PLAYED WITH MICROPHONES. WENT FOR A CYCLE.

6 FRIDAY: DAD STARTED CUTTING AFTER TEA. COLD WIND, DRY.

7 SATURDAY: HAD BAD HEADACHE ALL DAY, DID NOT DO MUCH. BURNLEY BEAT EVERTON, SPURS LOSE 7-2.

SEPTEMBER 1963

8 SUNDAY: STILL HAVE HEADACHE. GOT READY FOR SCHOOL. EDWARD FELL ON STONES AND CUT HIS LIP BADLY. BARRY AND NEIL CAME DOWN.

9 MONDAY: WENT UP TO VILLAGE. WENT UP THE CHURCH TOWER. WATCHED COMBINE WORKING. GOT STUFF READY FOR SCHOOL.

10 TUESDAY: BEGIN SCHOOL, WITH ROGER. NEW FORM MASTER. DAD BINDERS FIELD.

11 WEDNESDAY: DAD, DAVE, CHARLIE AND JOE FINISH ONE CORN FIELD. PLAYED IN SCHOOL TRIALS.

12 THURSDAY: PLAYED FOR 3rd YEAR IN SCHOOL, LEFT BACK, WON 3-0. COMBINED THE OTHER FIELD. HOT.

13 FRIDAY: VERY HOT. ROGER IS IN NELSON HOUSE IN SCHOOL, SO IS NEIL. DAD BALED, WE TIED BALES.

14 SATURDAY: HOPKINS LEAVE. MR HOPKINS GIVES ME TANKS FOR HORACE, MRS HOPKINS GIVES ME £1. DAD BALED, WE GOT IN SOME BALES.

On the Monday 9th of September in 1963 I stood with my mother at the top of our village church tower. I was thinking about the start of the new school term which would start the next day.

It was the end of the long school summer holiday and near the end of harvest time. The late summer sun beat down on the old lead panels of the tower, and between the lichen-encrusted stones we looked out at the circle of the parish before us.

Below, the cottages and houses of the village huddled towards the church, and further out, past the gateways and lanes was the age-old pattern of fields, some dotted with sheep or cattle, some golden with newly-cut corn. In between them the green woods folded into valleys. Further away the northern foothills and and the skyline of Exmoor, bronze age barrows on the spine of the highest hill, and to the south we saw the blue tors of Dartmoor.

I watched a red combine harvester slowly working its way around a corn field, the sound of men and machines muffled by distance, a dust cloud around them as it cut and gathered up the standing corn.

It was a similar machine that would work later in the week on our farm where the corn left behind would be gathered up by my father's orange Allis-Chalmers baler, producing small round straw bales which we still had to tie up with binder cord as we followed along behind it.

Although mostly mechanised now, the harvesting process was still the same as it had been for our ancestors, from the time of Beocca the Saxon who gave his name to

Bill Pidler and helper harvesting apples in the orchard at Witherhill Farm.

the village and farmed this land with his men. They would celebrate the end of harvest as we would, and the spirit of the corn. Below me in the dim light of the church this repeating story was shown in the carvings of wood and stone, in the decorative patterns of flowers, foliage, corn, and the intertwining ivy leaves around the head of the Green Man.

In the churchyard below some girls were playing around the headstones, while a cat lay sunbathing on a low grey stone wall.

We could see Mrs Tucker and Mrs Snell chatting outside the post office, and coming out of their cottage there was Jean Tapscott with her son Neil, who was the same age as my younger brother. Neil would in later years become a very successful hairdresser, with salons in Windsor and New York. Among his clients were royalty and many well-known personalities. When the singer Iris Williams was in concert in Moscow she flew him there to style her hair. Tragically Neil was killed when still a young man, in a car crash near his home at Windsor.

At around this time our neighbours Mr and Mrs Hopkins of Nethergrove Farm moved away. Good friends of my parents, they gave me a present of £1 and a tank for Horace, my goldfish.

The end of the week would finish with the annual trip to Barnstaple Fair. The noise and lights, the smell of hot dogs, candy floss and dodgems were, for a day at least, a welcome contrast to life in a quiet country village.

At a beach in the summer of 1963.

On the Saturday of that week the church would be decorated by the ladies of the village who would come with bundles of flowers, fruit and vegetables, and on the Sunday the church would resound to the hearty singing of the traditional harvest festival hymns.

As we made our way down the dusty tower into the dark silent coldness of the church, however, and out into the bright sunshine, all that was still in the days to come.

By now the sun was beginning its slow downward course and we walked home along the shaded lanes, past the orchards heavy with fruit, and cows at the gate now ready for milking time. I was thinking of getting prepared for tomorrow, the new school term, new teachers and meeting old classmates, as a cool breeze from the north slipped silently across the fields, rattled the beech trees above us and tumbled down the first leaves of Autumn.

Wards Cottage, with thatched roof, in 1958.

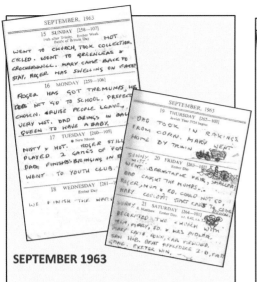

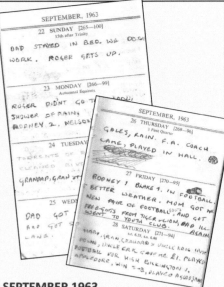

SEPTEMBER 1963

15 SUNDAY: WENT TO CHURCH, TOOK
COLLECTION. WENT TO GREENLEAS AND
CROCKERNWELL.

16 MONDAY: ROGER HAS MUMPS.
PREFECTS CHOSEN. CRUISE PEOPLE LEAVE.
DAD BRINGS IN BALES. QUEEN TO HAVE A
BABY.

17 TUESDAY: MISTY AND HOT. PLAYED 2
GAMES FOOTBALL. DAD FINISHED
BRINGING IN BALES. WENT TO YOUTH
CLUB.

18 WEDNESDAY: WE FINISH THE CORN
HARVEST.

19 THURSDAY: DAD TAKES IN CORN
RAKINGS. MARY WENT HOME BY TRAIN.

20 FRIDAY: SUNNY, MIST. WENT TO
BARNSTAPLE FAIR, SMALLER. DAD
CAUGHT THE MUMPS. MARY COULDN'T
START CAR.

21 SATURDAY: SUNNY, MARY CAME DOWN,
CAR MENDED. DECORATED THE CHURCH
WITH MUM, MARY, EDWARD AND MRS
PIDLER. EXETER WIN.
H.B. BEAT APPLEDORE 2-0.

SEPTEMBER 1963

22 SUNDAY: DAD STAYED IN BED. WE DO
THE WORK.

23 MONDAY: SHOWER OF RAIN. RODNEY 2
NELSON 2.

24 TUESDAY: TORRENTS OF RAIN. NO
FOOTBALL. CLEANED BIKE. GRAN,
GRANDAD AND MARY CAME DOWN.

25 WEDNESDAY: DAD GOT UP, DOCTOR
CAME, AND GOT STUCK AT END OF LANE.

26 THURSDAY: GALES, RAIN. F.A. COACH
CAME, PLAYED IN HALL.

27 FRIDAY: RODNEY 1 BLAKE 1 IN
FOOTBALL. BETTER WEATHER. MUM GOT
ME NEW PAIR OF FOOTBALL BOOTS AND
NEW GIFTS FROM TIGER & LION. DAD ILL
AGAIN. WENT TO YOUTH CLUB.

28 SATURDAY: MARY, GRAN, GRANDAD &
UNCLE ERIC CAME DOWN. UNCLE ERIC
GAVE ME £1. PLAYED FOOTBALL FOR HIGH
BICKINGTON v APPLEDORE, WIN 5-3,
PLAYED A GOOD GAME.

NOTES FOR SEPTEMBER 1963:

2ⁿᵈ Haircuts (originally short back and sides for 6d) were done by Mr Farley in the village.

3ʳᵈ Barry and Keith were Barry Tapscott and Keith Tucker.

11ᵗʰ Joe was Joe Tucker from the village.

16ᵗʰ The cruise was organised by the school for some pupils. The Queen's baby would be Prince Edward.

25ᵗʰ The doctor then was Doctor Cramp.

27ᵗʰ Tiger and Lion were very popular childrens comics. The Tiger featured "Roy of the Rovers."

30ᵗʰ Arthur J. Plummer had been the vicar of High Bickington since 1945, and was still the vicar there when I got married at the church in 1972.

Edward in the front garden at Witherhill, probably in 1962.

After a week of heavy rain in the last days of September the sun came out, and I sat in the hallway trying on my new football boots. My father was still in bed recovering from the mumps which has spread through the whole village. The doctor had visited the day before and on the way out got his car stuck at the end of the farm lane.

Left: Uncle Eric Warren and Aunt Gwen.

My grandparents and my aunt had visited us in the week to help out, and had arrived again this weekend. This time they came with Uncle Eric. (Eric Warren had married my grandmother's first cousin Gwen in 1931, and they were always affectionately known as Uncle and Auntie). Eric was a larger-than-life character, a Bertie Wooster type, smartly dressed with shiny shoes and a carnation in his lapel. He was a chatty, extrovert Londoner, quite different from the quiet, restrained family he had married into. My mother (called Hazel) was nicknamed "Nuts" and my nervous unmarried aunt Mary was relentlessly teased about potential male friends, and Eric liked telling us the story of how she was stopped from seeing a young farmer because her mother (my grandmother) didn't think he was at all good enough.

Gwen had passed away some years before but I have memories of her having tea, reminding her husband about his table manners, dressed in furs and pearls. I have a lovely photograph of her and her frail younger sister Elizabeth enjoying a picnic in the dappled sunshine of a warm, peaceful Edwardian day. Gwen and my grandmother's family were Aclands. The Acland family, possibly Flemish in origin, who had arrived at the time of the the the Norman conquest and in 1155 claimed the lands of Acca the Saxon who held large estates overlooking the Taw estuary in North Devon. All Aclands can trace their line back to this time and place. The family were fortunate to marry well and in the 16th century a branch of the family moved south to a property which would later become the Killerton estate.

In 1915 Gwen had married a 29-year-old farmer called William Tucker, but in just three months he was found dead from gunshot wounds. At his inquest Gwen is recorded as saying his death must have been an accident, she knew nothing to suggest otherwise. On the morning he had taken letters from the postman, but he himself had nothing in the post. Miss Perkins, of the household staff, said he told her he had seen a rabbit in the hedge and was going out to shoot it. Later a carpenter called Mr Fairfield saw a man lying on his back in the road, a gun across his left hip. He went to the house and asked for Mr Tucker and found he was not there. He went for the constable. When he went back he saw the man was dead, the top part of his head being blown off. PC Jarvis said the body was 170 paces from the house. There was a gap in the hedge and signs someone had gone through it.

There were footprints of the deceased, and a stick was produced that had broken from the hedge and found near the body. Dr Mitchell said the wound was such as might be caused by the gun being held a foot away. The jury returned a verdict of accidental death.

Gwen then went to work as a house-keeper for a gentleman in London. Following his death she met Eric and they spent all their married life in Wimbledon. He worked as a salesman for Huntley and Palmer's Biscuits, and following his retirement and Gwen's death, was very surprised that she had invested her money wisely and he had become an extremely wealthy man. His life without Gwen was spent on summers in English hotels, usually on the coast, and winters abroad on long holidays or a cruise. I remember, as a young teenager, staying with him and my Aunt Mary in a hotel in Reigate. We took tea in smoke-filled, genteel dining rooms, and visited the local park, the *Daily Telegraph* always under his arm. He offered to take us to a show in London and I would have quite liked to see Barbra Streisand, but we settled instead for *The Black and White Minstrel Show*.

As the years took their toll he spent his last days in just one room in a residential home in Exeter. We visited him and went again through his many photographs of holidays past. Always looking for the best in life he pointed out the bird-table in the garden, the cathedral tower beyond the houses, and the green fields just visible in the far distance from his chair by the window.

We left him eventually, to his tea and *Daily Telegraph,* as the pale sun dropped behind the grey, wet roof-tops of the city.

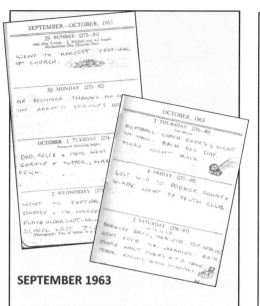

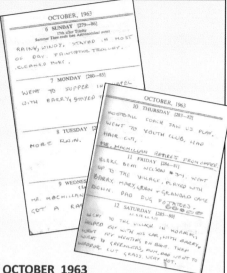

SEPTEMBER 1963

29 SUNDAY: WENT TO THE HARVEST FESTIVAL IN CHURCH.

30 MONDAY: MR PLUMMER THANKS ME FOR THE HARVEST SERVICES POSTERS.

OCTOBER 1963

1 TUESDAY: DAD, MUM, ROGER GO TO HARVEST SERVICE AND SUPPER. MARY CAME DOWN.

2 WEDNESDAY: WENT TO EXETER WITH DAD, BARRY AND MR MARDON. SAW EXETER PLAY ALDERSHOT, 0-0. SCHOOL LOST 7-2.

3 THURSDAY: FOOTBALL COACH COMES, WENT IN HALL. RAIN ALL DAY. MARY WENT BACK.

4 FRIDAY: LOST 4-0 TO RODNEY. SUNNY & WINDY. WENT YOUTH CLUB.

5 SATURDAY: BURNLEY DREW, MAN. UTD. - TOP LEAGUE. WENT OVER TO MR LARAMY'S. PEOPLE ABOUT CHAIRS AND TV CAME. MADE RACING TRACK SCENERY.

OCTOBER 1963

6 SUNDAY: RAINY, WINDY. STAYED IN MOST OF DAY. PAINTED TROLLEY, CLEANED BIKE.

7 MONDAY: WENT TO SUPPER IN CHAPEL WITH BARRY, STAYED TO THE SALE.

8 TUESDAY: MORE RAIN.

9 WEDNESDAY: MR MACMILLAN GOES TO HOSPITAL. GOT A RASH ON MY MOUTH.

10 THURSDAY: FOOTBALL COACH SAW US PLAY. WENT TO YOUTH CLUB. HAD HAIR CUT. MR MACMILLAN RETIRES FROM OFFICE.

11 FRIDAY: BLAKE BEAT NELSON 3-1. WENT UP TO VILLAGE, PLAYED WITH BARRY. MARY, GRAN AND GRANDAD CAME DOWN. DAD DUG POTATOES.

12 SATURDAY: WENT TO VILLAGE IN MORNING. HELPED BOY WITH CAR, WITH BARRY. WENT FOX HUNTING ON BIKE. THEN WENT TO GREENLEAS, MUM & DAD WENT TO A WEDDING. CUT GRASS. VERY HOT.

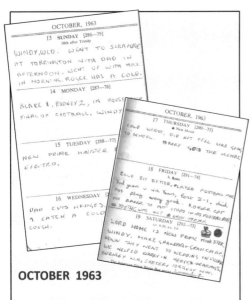

OCTOBER 1963

13 SUNDAY: WINDY, COLD. WENT TO
SCRAMBLE AT TORRINGTON WITH DAD IN
AFTERNOON. WENT UP WITH MILK IN
MORNING. ROGER HAS A COLD.

14 MONDAY: BLAKE 1 RODNEY 2 IN
HOUSE CUP FINAL OF FOOTBALL, WINDY,
RAIN.

15 TUESDAY: NEW PRIME MINISTER BEING
ELECTED.

16 WEDNESDAY: DAD CUTS HEDGES. I
CATCH A COLD, EAR-ACHE & COUGH.

17 THURSDAY: COLD WORSE. DID NOT
FEEL LIKE GOING TO SCHOOL. BARRY GETS
THE MUMPS.

18 FRIDAY: COLD A BIT BETTER. PLAYED
FOOTBALL FOR 3rd YEARS v 4th YEARS,
LOST 2-1, DID NOT PLAY VERY GOOD.
YOUTH CLUB NOT OPEN TODAY.

19 SATURDAY: LORD HOME IS NEW PRIME
MINISTER. WINDY. MARY, GRANDAD &
GRAN CAME DOWN, THEY WENT TO
WEDDING IN VILLAGE. WE HELP CARRY IN
HEDGE PARINGS. BURNLEY, EXETER WIN.

As the autumn of 1963 began, a spell of
wet and windy weather swept in from the
Atlantic and over the farm. The first
weekend of the month would see me
inside working on my balsa-wood glider,
painting a home-made go-kart, or cleaning
my bike.

On the first Wednesday of the month we
went to watch Exeter City play Aldershot at
St James Park. We took Grady (Wilfred)
Mardon, who worked at the village
butcher's, and who complained about the
appearance of the Rolling Stones on the
television that week and their daft songs.
We stood on the cold, damp terraces
watching an uneventful goal-less draw.
At the final whistle, we trooped out into

Aged 9 or 10 years old at Witherhill Farm.

Chulmleigh School Football Team 1964/5

the crush of grey hats and coats and a thick blanket of cigarette and pipe-smoke hanging in the damp early evening air.

I caught a bad cold the following week, and although not feeling like school, I played football. I struggled with no energy, playing badly, and my team-mate Roy Andrews made sure that I knew it.

However, football was a passion then and we always wanted to play - and in all weathers. Bad weather could mean a cancellation and be replaced with country-dancing in the school-hall and, worse still, with girls we could not choose to dance with. One day we all stood in the freezing rain all ready and willing to play, when our furious sports teacher Mr Davies held out his hands to catch the driving sleet and asked "What do you think this is - Scotch mist?". No-one answered. In the freezing cold we would still play...finally coming inside to grip the cloakroom's warm pipes and unlock our frozen fingers.

The Autumn chill brought the leaves down, horse-chestnuts were gathered for playing conkers, and the pheasant-shooting season began. The full-grown hedges of the country lanes were cut back, and we collected the parings to go on the bonfire. Mumps was still rife in the village, a number of my friends were down with it along with the village schoolmaster.

In the national news the Prime Minister, Harold Macmillan, had gone into hospital and later resigned. Sir Alec Douglas-Home was elected Prime Minister - the last holder of that office to be a member of the House of Lords and the only one to have played first class cricket - but the Conservative government, badly damaged by the Profumo scandal, could not survive.

Although at my age the Profumo and Christine Keeler story passed me by, the fall-out from the scandal represented a huge change in the cultural life of Britain.

As the evenings darkened I'd spend more time indoors, usually in a room we called the billiard-room because in its centre was a three-quarter-sized Edwardian billiard table my father had bought at a local sale. Despite its faded baize and hardened cushions it was still possible to use, which I did for hours on end.

This room with its thick stone and cob walls was the oldest part of the house, dating from the 15th century, and was sunk deep into the north-facing hillside. The house name Witherhill was originally Nitherhill or Netherhill, meaning "under the hill".

Above the billiard-room was my bedroom, and my parents' bedroom, and between the two was a small room my mother used to call the lumber room, which was full of old books, comics, clothes, an old desk and things that should have been thrown out years ago. Although we never talked about it this room had a rather strange, uncomfortable atmosphere, and we rarely played in there. It was not helped by it having a very small side-room or box-cupboard which my mother had curtained off, which had no window or light.

Many years later a new owner of the farmhouse asked if we had ever heard voices coming from that part of the house. My mother did once recall that my father said that when he went downstairs late one night he'd seen the shape of an old lady in the doorway of the hallway (what would have the original back door). The ancient farmhouse certainly had plenty of ghosts for those who could, or wanted to, see them.

The final night of the month of course was Hallow'een which coincided then with a full moon, but in those days there were no big carved pumpkins, no 'trick or treating', and no cheap plastic decorations.

Temperance Lloyd, Mary Trembles and Susannah Edwards of Bideford, the last women to be hanged for witchcraft in England, had lived only thirteen miles away as the crow flies.

Outside in the dark woods owls would call from the oak trees and dogs would bark to each other from farm to farm across the valley, and I would close the bedroom curtains against the cold glass and the black embrace of the night.

A rear view of Witherhill farm in the 1970s.

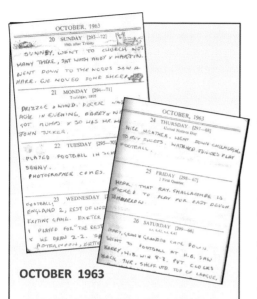

OCTOBER 1963

20 SUNDAY: SUNNY. WENT TO CHURCH, NOT MANY THERE. SAT WITH ANDY & MARTIN. WENT DOWN TO THE WOODS. SAW A HARE. WE MOVED SOME SHEEP.

21 MONDAY: DRIZZLE AND WIND. ROGER HAS STOMACH ACHE. BARRY AND NEIL STILL GOT MUMPS, SO HAS MR HARVEY AND JOHN TUCKER.

22 TUESDAY: PLAYED FOOTBALL IN SCHOOL. PHOTOGRAPHER COMES.

23 WEDNESDAY: FOOTBALL: ENGLAND 2 REST OF WORLD 1, VERY EXCITING GAME. EXETER WIN 5-0. I PLAYED FOR "REST" v SCHOOL TEAM, DRAW 2-2.

24 THURSDAY: NICE WEATHER. WENT DOWN TO CHULMLEIGH TO BUY SWEETS. WATCHED JUNIORS PLAY FOOTBALL.

25 FRIDAY: HEAR THAT RAYMOND SMALLACOMBE IS PICKED TO PLAY FOR EAST DEVON TOMORROW.

26 SATURDAY: MARY, GRAN AND GRANDAD CAME DOWN. WENT TO FOOTBALL AT H.B., SAW BARRY. H.B. WIN 8-3. PUT CLOCKS BACK 1 HOUR.

NOTES FOR OCTOBER 1963:

10th Harold Macmillan was the Prime Minister of Great Britain from 1957 to 1963.

13th Milk was delivered from us to Mrs Hare at Ward's Cottage.

14th Alexander Douglas-Home served as Prime Minister from October 1963 to October 1964.

20th Andy and Martin were Andrew and Martin Snell of High Bickington.

25th Raymond (and brother Colin) Smallacombe lived at Natson Farm, Bow.

27th Mr Ponsford lived at Stone Farm, Bridestowe, near Okehampton.

29th Slag, a by-product of the iron and steel industry, was spread on the fields.

A photograph of Shoplands, in the 1970s. Taken from the 'hen house' at Witherhill.

An ancient inscription in a Mid Devon vicarage reads...

" Bless this house, from wicked wight,
From Nightmare and the Goblin Light;
Goodfellow Robin, keep it from all evil
spirites, Fayries, Wezles, Bats and Ferryts;
From Curfew time till morn's Prime."

On the first day of November, All Saint's Day, we awoke to a grey wet morning. Our neighbour rang us to say her dog, a Boston Terrier, had given birth to a litter of puppies. In the afternoon we went to Exeter to buy fireworks for bonfire night. It was the time for village carnivals and fairs and with bonfire night, a link to the old tradition of raising light and music to brighten up the darkest time of the year, and call the warm sun back.

The following weekend I stayed at my grandparents' house. In their village they held an annual fair with a carnival in the evening. Traditionally, a Carnival Queen is chosen from the village girls, an echo of a much older ritual. This year she was someone I knew slightly, a farmer's daughter, blue-eyed and blonde. I watched her on her throne of flowers, her white dress, tiara and sequins sparkling in the November night. I suppose she was my first teenage infatuation. I went home with my parents that night and never saw her again, but I kept a newspaper cutting of her for almost a year.

At this time mains electricity was on its way to the farm. Before that the house got its electricity from a small generator which stood in the corner of a dusty barn which on its upper floor had a granary for storing grain. Below was the corn grinder which would crush the grain into animal feed. My father told us how, as a young man, he had caught one of his fingers in the grinding cogs. It was severed and landed on the floor. He liked to say he saw the farm cat running off with it. The large spinning wheel of the generator also proved a potential danger and one day my father caught my brother and I daring to touch it with a long stick. Luckily we got a good telling-off and a guard was made for it. An electrician, Cliff England, from the village, finished the rewiring of the house in readiness for the mains supply. During his work there he had gone off to have his lunch only to find my brother Edward, only a toddler then, had opened his lunch box and finished off most of his sandwiches.

Guy Fawkes Night was always a special date. We would have a big bonfire of the hedge cuttings in the orchard, and all around fires could be seen in the nearby villages and farms. One year we went to Lee Barton farm for firework night, and Richard Tucker put a lit firework on the open window-sill of their farmhouse kitchen where the mothers were preparing food. It went off with an almighty bang, and he was soon running past us down the lane with his father John in hot pursuit. It was sometime later they both appeared out of the dark, red-faced but laughing. It was always fun the next day finding the remnants of fireworks and throwing them back on to the smouldering bonfire to see what would happen.

My grandfather Charles Keen was born on the 1ˢᵗ June 1890 at Cliff Cottages near Exminster, and went to school there. The family moved to Glebe Farm, Kenn, and later to Lambert Farm at Crockernwell, near Cheriton Bishop. There he met Ellen Vigers and they got married on Christmas Eve at Cheriton Bishop church at 8.30 in the morning. He worked on the farm at Lambert, then moved to Walson Wood in Colebrooke, to Croft Farm in Spreyton and later to West Begbeer Farm near Bow. He died on the 12ᵗʰ April 1960 at Cheriton Bishop.

Ellen Vigers, born 10ᵗʰ June 1885. Went to school at Cheriton Bishop. Apprenticed to Miss Stanbury at Rose Cottage, Crockernwell. Went to London as a ladies maid to a clergyman's family. Returned through homesickness in 1901 and started her own dressmaking business, often working for estate houses such as Great Fulford. She married Charles Keen in 1910. Her daughter Phyllis Mary was born at Pocombe Cottage, Cheriton Bishop, on 25ᵗʰ May 1911. Her son, Samuel George was born on the 15ᵗʰ January 1922. She died 4ᵗʰ December 1968.

On the coming Saturday we went to Winkleigh Carnival and Fair. We visited great Uncle Frank and his sister, great Aunt Nell (Haydon) at Easton Barton, on the Sunday. From there we brought back a sixteenth-century oak chest, the family Bible and two framed photographs of my grandmother and grandfather, Charles and Ellen Keen (Vigers). Uncle Frank married his second wife Amy in 1963.

The following weekend I took the collection at church for the first time. That week was subjected to gales, heavy rain and flooding. On the Friday I got a new chess set which I had started to enjoy playing.

But it was whilst I was playing billiards one late afternoon in November that my mother came in to say that President Kennedy had been shot dead in the USA.

Members of the Pidler family who lived at Witherhill Farm from the 1920s to 1950s. Bill Pidler (top picture) and Phyllis Pidler.

It was very similar to the time when she had come into my bedroom in February 1958 to tell me about the Munich air crash, but I was well aware this was even worse news. Kennedy was part of the new optimism and glamour of the early sixties and it was a reminder we could be entering a darker and more uncertain time. The previous year we had got used to his name during the Cuban missile crisis, when the world had teetered on the eve of destruction. During the negotiations a blockade of ships was put around Cuba.

We came into a music lesson one day and our nice teacher Mrs Stentiford, a short lady who walked with a slight limp, said a Russian ship had already been sunk. Tension was in the air, and we worried about what would happen in the days ahead or whether we would even live to see them. The knowledge that the escalation of the crisis would mean almost total destruction for both sides meant Kennedy and Khrushchev pulled back from the brink of war.

The weapons were removed from Cuba, and eventually the US would remove its weapons from Turkey, but the fear of nuclear annihilation hung like a cloud over our generation and helped shape the attitudes of the sixties and beyond.

On the last Sunday in November, with the world still in shock, Lee Harvey Oswald, the man accused of the assassination, was shot dead in front of the world's cameras.

I wrote in my diary for that day:
"... the man accused of the President's death was shot dead. Went down to the woods. Nice weather".

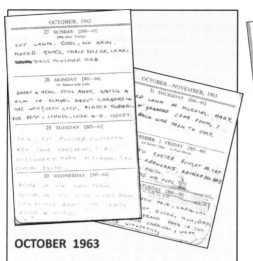

OCTOBER 1963

27 SUNDAY: UNCLE PONSFORD DIED.

28 MONDAY: WATCH FILM IN SCHOOL ABOUT CAREERS IN THE NAVY. PLAYED FOR REST v SCHOOL LOST 4-0. CLOUDY

29 TUESDAY: RAIN, BUT PLAYED FOOTBALL. MEN CAME SPREADING SLAG. MISSIONARY TALK IN SCHOOL. SAW SCHOOL DOCTOR.

30 WEDNESDAY: BROKE UP FOR HALF-TERM. GETTING ON WELL WITH MODEL PLANE. SAW SLIDES ABOUT THE SCHOOL CRUISE. RAIN & WIND.

31 THURSDAY: ROLLED LAWN IN MORNING. MARY, GRAN & GRANDAD CAME DOWN. I WENT BACK WITH THEM.

NOVEMBER 1963

1 FRIDAY: WENT TO EXETER, BOUGHT A LOT OF TOYS & FIREWORKS. RAINED ALL DAY. SAW PETER PARISH. MRS HARE'S DOG HAS PUPS.

2 SATURDAY: WENT TO BOW CARNIVAL & CROWNING OF QUEEN. MUM & DAD CAME IN NIGHT TO WATCH. WENT BACK HOME AT NIGHT.

NOVEMBER 1963

3 SUNDAY: TIRED. DID NOT DO MUCH. PAINTED MODEL CAR. PLAYED IN BILLIARD ROOM.

4 MONDAY: BARRY AND NEIL'S MUMPS BETTER AND CAME BACK TO SCHOOL. FLOODS NEAR RIVER.

5 TUESDAY: CROSS COUNTRY FOR GAMES. FIREWORK DAY. EDWARD WATCHED IT. MEN CAME TO SEE ABOUT BUYING ENGINE. CLIFF CAME, STARTING WIRING MAINS ELECTRIC IN HOUSE.

6 WEDNESDAY: WENT TO A JUMBLE SALE, DAD WENT TO FARM SALE AND BOUGHT A STOVE.

7 THURSDAY: CLIFF FINISHED INDOORS.

8 FRIDAY: MARY CAME DOWN. WENT TO YOUTH CLUB, 4 THERE. GOT PHOTOS, MUM BUYS MINE.

9 SATURDAY: TOOK MARY BACK. WENT TO FOOTBALL, H.B. WON 2-1. BURNLEY WIN, MAN. UTD. WIN. SAW WINKLEIGH CARNIVAL AND FAIR.

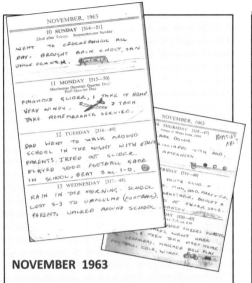

NOVEMBER 1963

10 SUNDAY: WENT TO CROCKERNWELL ALL DAY. BROUGHT BACK CHEST. SAW UNCLE FRANK.

11 MONDAY: FINISHED GLIDER. I TAKE IT HOME. VERY WINDY. 3 TECH TAKE A REMEMBRANCE SERVICE.

12 TUESDAY: DAD WENT TO WALK AROUND SCHOOL IN THE NIGHT WITH OTHER PARENTS. TRIED OUT GLIDER. PLAYED FOOTBALL IN SCHOOL.

13 WEDNESDAY: RAIN IN MORNING. SCHOOL LOST 5-3 TO UFFCULME. PARENTS WALKED AROUND SCHOOL.

14 THURSDAY: MARY CAME DOWN. PLAYED BILLIARDS WITH DAD. RAIN.

15 FRIDAY: WENT TO YOUTH CLUB AND JUMBLE SALE. MUM, DAD, MARY AND ED. WENT TO BARNSTAPLE. BOUGHT A LOT OF CARDS AT JUMBLE SALE. RAIN.

16 SATURDAY: CLEANED BIKES, MENDED ROGERS PUNCTURE. PLAYED BILLIARDS. WENT HARE HUNTING. TOOK MARY HOME, AND WATCHED BOW PLAY FOOTBALL. COLD, WINDY.

NOVEMBER 1963

17 SUNDAY: WENT TO CHURCH, TOOK COLLECTION. RAIN, GALE IN NIGHT.

18 MONDAY: VERY WINDY, RAIN. SPOKE ON A TAPE-RECORDER IN THE ENGLISH LESSON.

19 TUESDAY: DID NOT PLAY FOOTBALL. RAIN. RIVERS VERY HIGH, FLOODS. WENT A DIFFERENT WAY TO SCHOOL.

20 WEDNESDAY: WAS RESERVE FOR SCHOOL FOOTBALL TEAM, BUT GAME WAS CANCELLED BECAUSE OF FLOODS.

21 THURSDAY: ORDERED TECH DRAWING EQUIPMENT. WENT TO YOUTH CLUB. BARRY, ROGER AND I LIFTED TABLES INTO LOFT. RECORDED IT ON TAPE RECORDER, VERY COMICAL.

22 FRIDAY: MUM, DAD AND EDWARD WENT TO BARNSTAPLE. GOT NEW CHESS GAME. PRESIDENT KENNEDY SHOT DEAD IN TEXAS. HE WAS IN AN OPEN CAR WHEN HE WAS ASSASSINATED. USA SHOCKED.

23 SATURDAY: MARY, GRAN AND GRANDAD CAME DOWN. RICHARDS CAME TO VISIT US IN THE NIGHT, PLAYED WITH BOYS IN BILLIARD ROOM. MAN. UTD. LOSE, BURNLEY WIN.

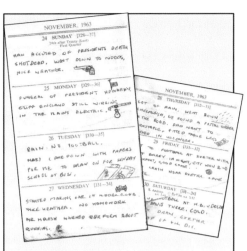

NOVEMBER 1963

24 SUNDAY: MAN ACCUSED OF
PRESIDENTS DEATH SHOT DEAD. WENT
DOWN TO WOODS. NICE WEATHER.

25 MONDAY: FUNERAL OF PRESIDENT
KENNEDY. CLIFF ENGLAND STILL WIRING
IN THE MAINS ELECTRIC.

26 TUESDAY: RAIN, NO FOOTBALL. MARY
CAME DOWN WITH PAPERS FOR ME TO
DRAW ON FOR SUNDAY SCHOOL AT BOW.

27 WEDNESDAY: STARTED MAKING CAR IN
MODEL CLUB. NICE WEATHER. NO
HOMEWORK. MR MARSH WARNS OUR
FORM ABOUT RUNNING.

28 THURSDAY: LOT OF RAIN. WENT DOWN
TO CHULMLEIGH, WE FOUND A POSTAL
ORDER ON ROAD. DAD WENT TO
BARNSTAPLE. FITTED TABLE LEGS
TOGETHER IN WOODWORK.

29 FRIDAY: WENT TO FOOTBALL AT
EXETER WITH DAD & BARRY IN NIGHT,
CITY WON 2-0 v STOCKPORT, GOOD
GAME. SAW A CRASH NEAR EXETER,
CAME HOME LATE.

30 SATURDAY: ENTRY BLANK.

NOTES FOR NOVEMBER 1963:

1st Peter Parish was a classmate from
Chawleigh. Mrs Hare's dog was a Boston
Terrier.

5th Cliff England was a local electrician, and
lived in North Road, High Bickington with his
wife Christine.

10th My father's uncle Frank Keen and his wife
Amy lived in Golden Lion Cottage, Crockernwell.
Amy's first husband was killed in a farm
accident. Frank farmed at Lambert Farm,
Crockernwell, and Thorne Farm, Bow. His first
wife was Lily Ruddall from Drewsteignton, and
they are buried together in Drewsteignton
churchyard.

11th The glider was made of balsa wood.

22nd President John F. Kennedy was
assassinated in Dallas, Texas, while he was
riding as a passenger in a Lincoln Continental
convertible automobile. He was accompanied
by his wife, Jacqueline Kennedy, Texas Governor
John Connally and the Governor's wife Nellie
Connally, Secret Service Agent Roy Kellerman,
and the driver, agent William Greer.

23rd The very first episode of 'Doctor Who' was
shown on BBC television. The Richards were
farmers from Heasley Mill near North Molton,
and sold us ewes and rams.

24th Lee Harvey Oswald, the accused assassin
of President Kennedy was shot on live television
and died later in hospital.

25th The state funeral of John F. Kennedy took
place in Washington, D.C.

On the first week of December 1963 a big change came to the farm. Mains electricity had arrived. In the previous five years we had got light and power from a generator that stood in a shed below the granary store called the engine house.

As soon as the mains was connected the old generator was sold and a world of possibilities opened up. The first thing my father did was get a big second-hand freezer. It was wheeled down into the dairy, a north-facing room with grey slate flooring, a small window and wooden benches all around. Normally food was kept there in a large cupboard with a thin metal mesh around it to keep out flies. On the side would often stand a large pan of scalded milk, ready to develop its thick yellow crust of clotted cream.

Aerial photograph of the farm in the 1960s.

With the arrival of the freezer came a large box of ice-creams, a rare luxury, and something to look forward to the next day after school. The engineer who installed the freezer was the father of John Tilson, my then best friend at school. He and his parents had moved down from Bedfordshire and John had struggled at first, but with the help of an inspirational teacher he had developed a passion for geography and geology, and his English and other subjects blossomed. Collecting rock samples became our new hobby. When his father had a job on in Cornwall he would take us down there and let us wander the cliffs of Tintagel and Boscastle, discovering the shining granite stones and the green serpentine.

On the way back, and nearly home, we would call in at John's father's local pub, a traditional hunting and fishing hotel in the woods of the Taw valley. We would sit in the corner with our lemonade and crisps, below cabinets filled with fishing trophies.

The landlord would eye up any strangers with a deep suspicion, and most teenagers with distaste. To his pals he would loudly recount the heroics of brave Spitfire pilots for youngsters like us to hear, and perhaps for him to hold back the unwelcome changes of the sixties.

The best field for stones on the farm was the highest around, and where an ancient ash tree stood on the hedge line, split open by lightning and bent almost double by Atlantic gales. The stones were a dull sandstone, but sometimes a glittering piece of quartz would catch the eye, or a chalk stone with an imprint of a delicate fern laid down on this land when it was a swamp in the age of the dinosaurs.

A view from the Witherhill fields, looking north to Exmoor.

From the tree we could see the high tors of Dartmoor to the south and the blue hills of Exmoor to the north. Below us the Taw valley, green woods criss-crossed by footpaths and small roads connecting the farms still with their ancient Celtic and Saxon names, Dadland, Seckington, Gratley, Deptford, Shuteley and Snape.

In times gone past these old track ways and footpaths were imprinted on the memories of the children of the parish during the tradition of "beating the bounds". Elders would walk with youngsters, showing them the boundaries of the parish and impressing on them the dangers of straying "out of bounds" or going beyond their limits.

I had come home from school on the 11th looking forward to ice cream but found my disgruntled parents clearing out the freezer. It had not worked, everything had melted and was being thrown out. My mother and father, as usual, spoke of their bad luck, of things forever going wrong for them and how they should always "expect the worse". I think some of this might have come from their early life together when,

soon after the war and their wedding, my mother was expecting a baby. All was going fine until the actual birth when something went wrong and a baby girl was stillborn. No one ever talked about it, as people didn't then, and I never asked. Looking through some papers after my mother's death I found a receipt from Whites the undertakers for "making an oak coffin and burying an infant, fifteen shillings and sixpence". So somewhere in a Crediton churchyard lies my sister.

John's father called the next day and repaired the freezer, it was a simple fault. We came home from school and although there were no ice-creams the freezer was full of meat, a good insurance policy after the previous long and bitter winter.

My father had also been out and bought a second-hand television and, although he still had to go up a ladder to the roof and adjust the aerial, it had a much better picture than the last one.
So, with a good television set, my birthday coming up, and a large turkey ordered for the freezer, all seemed well and ready for Christmas Day.

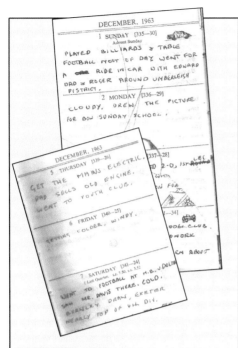

DECEMBER 1963

1 SUNDAY: PLAYED BILLIARDS AND TABLE FOOTBALL MOST OF DAY. WENT FOR A RIDE IN CAR WITH DAD, ROGER AND EDWARD AROUND UMBERLEIGH AND DISTRICT.

2 MONDAY: CLOUDY. DREW THE PICTURE FOR BOW SUNDAY SCHOOL.

3 TUESDAY: BLANK ENTRY.

4 WEDNESDAY: BLANK ENTRY.

5 THURSDAY: GET THE MAINS ELECTRIC. DAD SELLS THE OLD ENGINE. WENT TO YOUTH CLUB.

6 FRIDAY: GETTING COLDER. WINDY.

7 SATURDAY: WENT TO FOOTBALL AT H.B. V DOLTON. SAW MR DAVIS THERE. COLD. BURNLEY DRAW. EXETER NEARLY TOP OF 4th DIV.

DECEMBER 1963

8 SUNDAY: DID NOT GO TO CHURCH. STILL VERY COLD.

9 MONDAY: MAN. UTD. BEAT SPURS 4-1, AND WIN ON AGGREGATE. DAVE MACKAY BREAKS HIS LEG.

10 TUESDAY: GOT THE DEEP FREEZE AND ICE CREAMS. PLAYED FOOTBALL.

11 WEDNESDAY: DEEP FREEZE NOT WORKING PROPERLY, SO ICE-CREAMS MELT AND HAVE TO BE THROWN AWAY.

12 THURSDAY: MAN MENDS THE DEEP FREEZE AND WE PUT A LOT OF MEAT IN. BOUGHT A NEW TELEVISION, GOOD PICTURE.

13 FRIDAY: WENT TO THE YOUTH CLUB. PLAYED WITH TAPE RECORDER. COLD IN NIGHT.

14 SATURDAY: SAW H.B. PLAY CHULMLEIGH FOOTBALL, WIN 2-1. VERY COLD. BURNLEY AND MAN. UTD. WIN. CLEANED OUT FISH TANK.

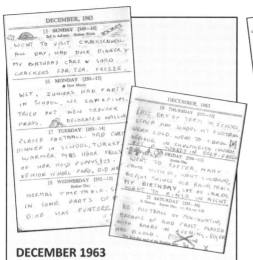

DECEMBER 1963

15 SUNDAY: WENT TO CROCKERNWELL ALL DAY, HAD DUCK DINNER & MY BIRTHDAY CAKE & GOOD CRACKERS FOR TEA. FREEZE.

16 MONDAY: WET. JUNIORS HAD A PARTY IN SCHOOL. DECORATED SCHOOL. TRIED OUT NEW TROUSER PRESS. SAW FILM.

17 TUESDAY: PLAYED FOOTBALL. HAD CHRISTMAS DINNER IN SCHOOL. MRS HARE SELLS ONE OF HER PUPPIES £23. SENIOR SCHOOL PARTY, DID NOT GO.

18 WEDNESDAY: NORMAL TIMETABLE. SNOW IN SOME PARTS OF BRITAIN. BIKE HAS A PUNCTURE.

19 THURSDAY: LAST DAY OF TERM. STAFF PLAY SCHOOL AT FOOTBALL. VERY COLD, WENT TO CAROL SERVICE AT CHULMLEIGH. PUT TURKEY IN DEEP FREEZE.

20 FRIDAY: 14 YEARS OLD. WENT TO EXETER. MARY WITH US, WENT SHOPPING. BOUGHT THINGS FOR RACING TRACK. LOT OF CARDS. WENT TO BINGO IN NIGHT.

21 SATURDAY: NO FOOTBALL OR FOX HUNTING BECAUSE OF BAD FROST.

DECEMBER 1963

22 SUNDAY: FROSTY. TOOK MARY TO STATION. DAD GOT A CHRISTMAS TREE, WE DECORATED IT. WROTE OUT POSTERS.

23 MONDAY: DAD, ROGER & I WENT TO BARNSTAPLE, SAW DECORATIONS IN STREETS. DAD TRIED OUT A VAUXHALL VELOX, IT WAS TOO BIG.

24 TUESDAY: DROVE IN SOME CALVES. CRUISE SHIP 'LAKONIA' SINKS. ICE, FROST.

25 WEDNESDAY: MARY, GRAN, GRANDAD & UNCLE ERIC COME FOR CHRISTMAS DINNER. BIG TURKEY. HAD MANY PRESENTS, CRAYONS, DIARY, BOOKS, CHESS & HALMA SETS.

26 THURSDAY: WENT TO GREENLEAS. VERY FOGGY & SLIPPERY ON ROADS, WENT SLOWLY. BURNLEY BEAT MAN. UTD. 6-1. EXETER 3rd IN LEAGUE.

27 FRIDAY: WET. CYCLED ABOUT. WROTE THANK-YOU LETTERS. PAINTED POLE.

28 SATURDAY: MEN SPREADING SLAG, GOT STUCK IN MUD. WENT TO FOOTBALL AT EXETER WITH UNCLE ERIC, THEY PLAYED BRIGHTON, 0-0.

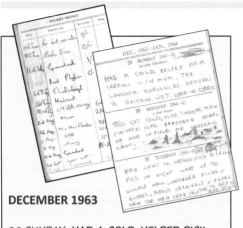

DECEMBER 1963

29 SUNDAY: HAD A COLD. HELPED PICK GREENS WITH MUM. THE LAKONIA SURVIVORS RETURN TO BRITAIN. WET. WAR IN CYPRUS.

30 MONDAY: STILL GOT COLD. SORE THROAT. MEN FINISHED SLAG, SPREAD HEAPS IN FIELD. MR UNDERHILL CAME.

31 TUESDAY: DAD WENT TO HATHERLEIGH TO SELL PIGS. IN NIGHT WENT UP TO VILLAGE HALL, WATCHED FILMS AND SLIDES ABOUT CARNIVALS AND FETES. SAW THE NEW YEAR IN. CAME TO BED AT ONE O'CLOCK.

NOTES FOR DECEMBER 1963:

Saturday 30th November and Tuesday and Wednesday 3rd and 4th of December are left blank as the page has been torn.

1st Our car at that time was a blue Austin A40 Somerset convertible, very unreliable but fun to be a passenger in.

2nd Bow Sunday School was held in the Bow Congregational Church Rooms. Mrs Lillian Job was in charge, with my aunt Mary helping. I went on most Sunday mornings when we lived at Greenleas.

7th Mr Davis was a history and PE teacher.

9th Dave Mackay was a member of the 'double' winning Tottenham side of 1961. He was later a manager at Derby County.

24th The Greek Line cruise ship TSMS Lakonia caught fire on the 22nd, and sank on the 29th. 128 people died. An electrical wiring fault had caused the fire.

Form 4A, Chulmleigh Secondary School 1965-1966

The 22nd of December 1963, the shortest day of the year. Down in the wood my father finds a small fir tree growing out of the brown leaf mould. Our Christmas tree. The dark night comes in early, freezing cold air hangs heavy over the farmhouse, and the smoking log fire struggles to get going. We bring down an old cardboard box and take out the well-used Christmas decorations. Home-made paper chains are hung over the table and cut holly is put around the fireplace.

During the night, as we sleep, hundreds of miles away, the Greek cruise ship *Lakonia* starts to sink into the sea. She is carrying 1000 people and 400 crew on board, mostly German and English. Many are enjoying a late-night party, and are in high spirits, when a fire breaks out on board. In the mass panic that follows lots of them choose to jump into the dark, cold water, many still in fancy dress and pyjamas. 128 people perished, mostly from the cold.

We go in to Barnstaple the next day to see the street lights and decorations. The small town's streets are packed with shoppers. My father tries out a Vauxhall Velox car, but thinks it is too big for us. On Christmas Eve we go up into the fields and drive the calves over the frozen turf into the barns.

As a new teenager I was becoming less excited about Christmas. I was no longer trying to peer through the window into the star-lit night sky, listening intently for sleigh bells, and trying to sleep before waking very early to the weight of a Christmas stocking on the bed. Now I'm settled under the blankets, my feet on a hot water bottle and a cat curled up asleep on the bed.

In the morning when I get up frost has decorated the cold glass window panes. My mother is already in the kitchen, peeling vegetables and preparing the large turkey. There are saucepans on the Rayburn with sprouts, carrots, parsnips and potatoes, and on the wood sideboard tangerines, nuts and dates. My father comes in from milking as my grandparents, aunt Mary and uncle Eric arrive for the day. After a good dinner, including a home-made Christmas pudding with clotted cream and a concealed sixpence, we open our presents. I have sketch books, crayons, a diary and a chess set. We watch television. The time is checked for three o'clock, time for a cup of tea, Christmas cake, and the message from the Queen.

On Boxing Day we drive down to Bow to see my grandparents. The roads are covered in black ice, and we drive very slowly home, following a thin line of 'cats eyes' in the freezing fog.

On the very last night of the year we went up to the Village Hall to watch a film and slide-show about 'Carnivals and Fetes'. After it had finished everyone enjoyed some refreshments, and a dance band played. Then, on the stroke of midnight, everybody welcomed in 1964, and we all said good-bye to a special year, 1963.

Looking towards Nethergrove from the lane at Witherhill.

A photograph from the Beaford Old Archive.

www.beafordoldarchive.org.uk

"And as I was green and carefree, famous among the barns

About the happy yard and singing as the farm was home,

In the sun that is young once only,

Time let me play and be

Golden in the mercy of his means,

And green and golden I was huntsman and herdsman, the calves

Sang to my horn, the foxes on the hills barked clear and cold,

And the sabbath rang slowly

In the pebbles of the holy streams".

An extract from the poem "Fern Hill" by Dylan Thomas

REFERENCE:

THE BOOK OF HIGH BICKINGTON. A Devon Ridgeway Parish.
By AVRIL STONE. Published by Halsgrove Publishing 2000

THE BEAFORD OLD ARCHIVE
www.beafordoldarchive.org.uk

A DEVON FAMILY. The Story of the Aclands.
By Anne Acland. Published by Phillimore & co. ltd. 1981